Preface

Exercises for *The Everyday Writer* is a resource for teachers and students. Its exercises consist of sentences and paragraphs needing revision, most of them designed so that students can edit directly on the pages of this book.

The exercise sets are numbered to correspond to chapters in *The Everyday Writer*, so that students can quickly locate help by following the cross-references in each exercise's instructions.

To help students check their own progress as they work, answers to the even-numbered exercise items appear in the back of this book. Exercises with many possible answers—those asking students to imitate a sentence or revise a paragraph, for example—are not answered here. Answers to the odd-numbered exercises are given in the instructor's answer key only.

If you have adopted *The Everyday Writer* as a text, you are welcome to photocopy any of these exercises to use for homework assignments, for classroom activities, or for quizzes. The book is also available for student purchase. Also available on our Web site are additional exercises for practice: <bedfordstmartins.com/everyday_writer>.

Preface

Contents

EXERCISES

THE EVERYDAY WRITER

EXERCISES

THE
EVERYDAY
WRITER

Third Edition

Lex Runciman

LINFIELD COLLEGE

Carolyn Lengel

BEDFORD/ST. MARTIN'S
BOSTON ◆ NEW YORK

Manufactured in the United States of America.

9 8 7 6 5
f e d c b a

For information, write: Bedford/St. Martin's, 75 Arlington Street,
Boston, MA 02116   (617-399-4000)

ISBN: 0-312-41972-4

EAN: 978-0-312-41972-1

LANGUAGE/GLOSSARY OF USAGE   74

PUNCTUATION/MECHANICS   92

FOR MULTILINGUAL WRITERS   121

ANSWERS TO THE EVEN-NUMBERED EXERCISES   135

EXERCISES

THE
EVERYDAY
WRITER

Learning from Common Errors

3.1 Recognizing and eliminating the twenty most common errors

Revise each of the following numbered items to eliminate one of the twenty most common sentence-level errors written by first-year students. (See *The Everyday Writer*, pp. 9–22.) Example:

> Learning another language is not a matter of genes; it's a matter of hard work.

1. Millie looked exhausted when she arrived from the airport. She sat her bags down in the hallway and stood there fanning her sweating face with her used plane ticket.

2. Today, we often forget how dangerous childhood diseases can be, less than a century ago, many children did not survive to adulthood because of diphtheria, whooping cough, and measles. Fortunately, such ailments are rare nowadays, however, if people decide not to immunize their children, these illnesses could easily make a comeback.

3. The Beast, which is one of the biggest roller coasters, has a thunderous ride of steep hills and turns. As you race down the first and biggest hill your coaster is engulfed by a tunnel at the end of the hill.

4. I was gaining speed and feeling really good but when I looked back he wasn't there. I panicked. I saw him and my parents down at the other end of the street and forgot to look forward. When I finally did turn forward, I saw that I was rapidly closing in on my neighbor's car.

5. I had to root for a World Series pitting the Chicago Cubs against the Boston Red Sox. Even though my brother, who believes that both teams

are historically cursed, was convinced that the world would end if either team won a pennant.

6. Trying to keep parents happy is a constant effort made by kids to keep in good standing with mom and dad. After all, it is they who will support us until we are capable of living on our own with things like money, food, and clothes.

7. After deciding to begin your college career, many students are then faced with the predicament of where to live. This matter is not such a problem for students from out of town, but it is if you live in the same city or area in which you chose a school.

8. The good thing about its location is that it is right off the main highway, very easy to spot. There are also plenty of road signs pointing you in the right direction of the park. And if you got extremely lost, pulling off and asking would be the easiest way to get on track.

9. My children turned up their noses at anything spicy until my twelve-year-old daughters friend Georgia asked for hot sauce at our dinner table recently. I called Georgias house the next day and thanked her for convincing my kids to try something new.

10. Once you find where other surfers are, you can set up your camp. This entails claiming your own territory. You do this by laying out your oversized beach towel and by turning your radio on loud enough to mark your domain without disturbing anyone else. This should help you blend in with the locals.

11. The car broke down on the highway, and we waited hours for a tow truck to arrive. We arrived to Marisol's house almost twenty hours late, but we still made it to the ceremony.

12. Determined to find the smartest dog possible, Ed searched pet stores across the entire state. He even named his new puppy Einstein, but that didn't prevent the dog from chasing it's tail.

13. Martin Luther King Jr. Day was a holiday for years in forty-nine states, but the fiftieth, New Hampshire, did not celebrate King Day until 2000. On June 7, 1999, Governor Jeanne Shaheen of New Hampshire had finally signed into law a bill making the holiday official.

14. Is student plagiarism such a problem that professors are justified in using Web sites such as plagiarism.com to check students' work? Those university representatives who argue that students and professors should rely on an honor system believes that investigating student essays does more harm than good.

15. Drivers in parts of the country where winters are mild may need to be reminded of what to do in case the car begins to slide on a patch of ice. They should stop pressing on the accelerator avoid braking, and steer in the direction of the skid.

16. The political discussions of "family values" do not take into account the fact that divorce is not always the worst outcome for children. A child in an extremely unhappy home will not necessarily be more miserable if their parents divorce.

17. I felt someone's hand shaking my shoulder. I lifted my head up to see my best friend, Stephanie, looking down at me. "That must have been some dream. Come on the bell rang class is over."

18. In the attic, we found several old board games, that no one remembered how to play. After we found the rules for Chinese checkers on a Web site, Grandma Jo asked us to show her how to use the Internet.

19. I decided to begin searching for an outfit while the rollers in my hair cooled. I began throwing everything out of my closet. Nothing fits my mood, and not one thing caught my eyes as they fell on the bed. I had no idea what I was even looking for since I didn't know where I was going.

20. The knights with armor and horses beautifully decorated participate in battles of jousting, target shooting with spears, archery, and duels of strategy and strength using swords and shields. During the evening, there is a break from the fighting, and a beautiful ceremony of marriage is acted out.

Composing in a Digital Age

10.1 Using the Toulmin system

Use the seven-part Toulmin system to begin to develop an argument for one of the following questions. Here is the Toulmin system:

1. Make your claim.
2. Restate or qualify your claim.
3. Present good reasons to support your claim.
4. Explain the underlying assumptions that connect your claim and your reasons. If an underlying assumption is controversial, provide backing for it.
5. Provide additional grounds to support your claim.
6. Acknowledge and respond to possible counterarguments.
7. Draw a conclusion, stated as strongly as possible.

(See *The Everyday Writer,* p. 73.)

1. Should the Pledge of Allegiance include the phrase "Under God," or should that phrase be omitted?

2. Should schools be responsible for children's moral education, or should a child's moral development be solely the concern of the parents?

10.2 Recognizing logical and emotional fallacies

Identify any logical or emotional fallacies in the sentences below. (Some sentences may contain both logical and emotional fallacies; others may not contain either.) If a passage contains a fallacy, indicate whether it is a logical fallacy, an emotional fallacy, or a combination of both, and then write out a sentence or two explaining your reasoning. If a sentence contains neither fallacy, write C. (See *The Everyday Writer,* pp. 73–76.) Example:

> **The boys listened to punk rock bands, so it wasn't surprising that they planned an attack on their schoolmates.**

Fallacy: _logical_____

Explanation: _Without offering any evidence, the sentence implies_____
that listening to punk rock bands caused the boys to plan the attack.

1. Two teenagers walked right past the woman who had fallen on
   the icy sidewalk. Young people today never lift a finger to help
   others.
   Fallacy: _____
   Explanation: _____

   _____

2. If schools don't get more financial help, Americans had better be
   prepared to live in a country run by dunces.
   Fallacy: _____
   Explanation: _____

   _____

3. Americans today are less likely than their counterparts thirty years
   ago to listen to local or regional music on the radio because radio
   stations in the United States, which once supported local artists,
   today are unlikely to play songs that do not have nationwide distribu-
   tion.
   Fallacy: _____
   Explanation: _____

   _____

4. Children who grow up with computers will be assured of lucrative
   careers someday.
   Fallacy: _____
   Explanation: _____

   _____

5. Most of the girls in the local high school have their hair in bangs this year. Any girl who wants to be liked should cut her hair the same way.

   Fallacy: _____

   Explanation: _____

   _____

6. Low self-esteem often leads to poor performance in school. Several studies show that teenagers who have low self-esteem tend to get bad grades.

   Fallacy: _____

   Explanation: _____

   _____

7. If marijuana can help terminally ill patients, then it should be legalized for recreational use.

   Fallacy: _____

   Explanation: _____

   _____

8. A survey of National Rifle Association members showed that Americans will offer tremendous resistance to laws making any restrictions on their right to bear arms.

   Fallacy: _____

   Explanation: _____

   _____

9. Girls are much better behaved than boys. My five-year-old daughter never breaks things or screams like her four-year-old cousin James does.

   Fallacy: _____

   Explanation: _____

   _____

10. A beautiful smile like yours deserves the finest toothpaste money can buy.

Fallacy: _____

Explanation: _____

_____

11.1   Recognizing arguable statements

Indicate which of the following sentences are arguable statements of opinion and which are factual by filling in the blank after each sentence with *arguable* or *factual*. (See *The Everyday Writer,* pp. 79–80.) Example:

The eradication of smallpox was the most important medical advance of the twentieth century.   <u>arguable</u>

1. Every student should learn about the ravages of smallpox. _____

2. Smallpox killed at least a third of its victims throughout recorded history. _____

3. No disease could ever be more frightening than smallpox was to people five hundred years ago. _____

4. Smallpox decimated the native populations in the Americas during the era of European exploration and colonization. _____

5. Some scholars believe that the European explorers purposefully infected native people with smallpox. _____

6. Columbus and other explorers must have realized that the people in the New World could have no immunity to European diseases. _____

7. The European interlopers and their virus destroyed cultures that were vastly superior to their own. _____

8. The World Health Organization declared in 1958 that eradicating smallpox was a worthy goal. _____

9. Smallpox, the first disease to be wiped out by human efforts, was declared dead in 1980. _____

10. The samples of smallpox virus currently kept alive in maximum-security freezers should not be destroyed because terrorist groups might also store the virus. _____

11.2 Demonstrating fairness

Study carefully the following advertisement for a mutual fund. Then, answer each of the following questions in a brief paragraph.

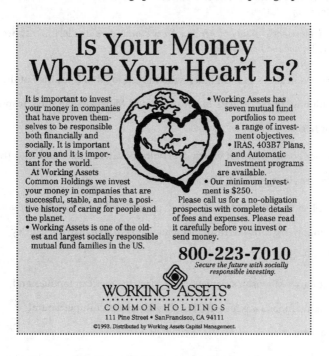

1. How do the copywriters establish common ground?

2. How do they demonstrate fairness?

3. How do they shape their appeal?

(See *The Everyday Writer*, pp. 82–83.)

Sentence Style

21.1 Matching subjects and predicates

Revise each of the following sentences in two ways to make its structures consistent in grammar and meaning. (See *The Everyday Writer,* pp. 184–185.) Example:

> **By studying African American folklore and biblical stories have influenced Toni Morrison's fiction.**
>
> African American folklore and biblical stories have influenced Toni Morrison's fiction.
>
> Toni Morrison's study of African American folklore and biblical stories has influenced her fiction.

1. Toni Morrison's grandmother, who moved to Ohio from the South with only fifteen dollars to her name, and Morrison had great respect for her.

2. In her books, many of which deal with the aftermath of slavery, often feature strong women characters.

3. Published in 1970, Morrison's first novel, *The Bluest Eye,* the story of a young African American girl who wants to look like her Shirley Temple doll.

4. Although Morrison's depictions of African American families and neighborhoods are realistic, but they also include supernatural elements.

5. An important character in Morrison's 1977 novel *Song of Solomon* is about Pilate, a woman with magical powers.

6. *Song of Solomon,* hailed as a masterpiece, winning the National Book Critics Circle Award in 1978.

7. Morrison's fame as a writer won the Pulitzer Prize in fiction in 1988 for *Beloved*.

8. The title character in *Beloved* features the ghost of a murdered infant inhabiting the body of a young woman.

9. When reading *Beloved* makes the horrors of American slavery seem immediate and real.

10. In 1993, Toni Morrison, who became the first African American woman to be awarded the Nobel Prize in literature.

21.2 Making comparisons complete, consistent, and clear

Revise each of the following sentences to eliminate any inappropriate elliptical constructions; to make comparisons complete, logically consistent, and clear; and to supply any other omitted words that are necessary for meaning. (See *The Everyday Writer*, p. 186.) Example:

Most of the candidates are bright, and one is brilliant.

1. Tim decided to take a nap, Michael decided to study for his chemistry test, and Susan to take a book back to the library.

2. New York City has a more diverse culture than any metropolis in the United States.

3. Laws governing drug use in Canada are more liberal than the United States.

4. As time went on, the baby became less animated and interested.

5. Argentina and Peru were colonized by Spain, and Brazil by Portugal.

6. The car's exterior is blue, but the seats black vinyl.

7. The house is Victorian, its windows enormous.

8. Are citizens of the United States now as safe or safer than they were before September 11, 2001?

9. My new stepmother makes my father happier.

10. She argued that children are even more important for men than women.

21.3 Revising for consistency and completeness

Revise this passage so that all sentences are grammatically and logically consistent and complete. (See *The Everyday Writer,* pp. 183–186.)

A concentrated animal feeding operation, or CAFO, is when a factory farm raises thousands of animals in a confined space. Vast amounts of factory-farm livestock waste, dumped into giant lagoons, which are an increasingly common sight in rural areas of this country. Are factory-farm operations healthy for their neighbors, for people in other parts of the country, and the environment? Many people think that these operations damage our air and water more than small family farms.

One problem with factory farming is the toxic waste that has contaminated groundwater in the Midwest. In addition, air quality produces bad-smelling and sometimes dangerous gases that people living near a CAFO have to breathe. When a factory farm's neighbors complain may not be able to close the operation. The reason is because most factory farms have powerful corporate backers.

Not everyone is angry about the CAFO situation; consumers get a short-term benefit from a large supply of pork, beef, and chicken that is cheaper than family farms can raise. However, the more people know about factory farms, the less interest in supporting their farming practices.

22.1 Combining sentences with coordination

Using the principles of coordination to signal equal importance or to create special emphasis, combine and revise the following twelve short sentences into several longer and more effective ones. Add or delete words as necessary. (See *The Everyday Writer,* pp. 186–190.)

The bull-riding arena was fairly crowded. The crowd made no impression on me. I had made a decision. It was now time to prove myself. I was scared. I walked to the entry window. I placed my money on the counter. The clerk held up a Stetson hat filled with slips of paper. I reached in. I picked one. The slip held the number of the bull I was to ride. I headed toward the stock corral.

22.2 Writing sentences with subordination

Combine each of the following sets of sentences into one sentence that uses subordination to signal the relationships among ideas. Add or delete words as necessary. (See *The Everyday Writer,* pp. 186–190.) Example:

The bus swerved to avoid hitting a dog.
It narrowly missed a car.
The car was in the bus driver's blind spot.

When the bus swerved to avoid hitting a dog, it narrowly missed a car that was in the bus driver's blind spot.

1. The scenery in the park is beautiful.

   The mountains have caps of snow.

   The lakes are deep and full of fish.

   The pastures are green.

   It is an ideal spot to spend spring break.

2. I spent a long night on a sleep sofa.

   I was at my parents' house.

The sleep sofa has an uncomfortably thin mattress with a hard metal bar beneath it.

3. Al Franken wrote a book about conservatives in American media.

Fox News filed a lawsuit to stop publication of the book.

The lawsuit was thrown out of court.

The book became a best-seller.

4. I walked into the shelter.

Men, women, and children were slumped against the wall.

Shopping carts containing families' belongings lay on their sides.

5. We had dug a seventy-foot ditch.

My boss would pour gravel into the ditch.

I would level the gravel with a shovel.

22.3 **Using coordination and subordination**

Revise the following paragraph, using coordination and subordination where appropriate to clarify the relationships between ideas. (See *The Everyday Writer*, pp. 186–190.)

Wasabi is a root. It originally came from Japan. Wasabi is prized as a spice. It can cost as much as $100 per pound. It is related to horseradish. Wasabi has the same sinus-clearing effect that horseradish has. It grows in icy mountain streams. Wasabi is difficult to grow on farms. American farmers are trying to perfect techniques for growing wasabi in this country. One Californian has invested in expensive technology for his wasabi farm. His name is Roy Carver. He is the largest producer of wasabi outside of Japan. People have tried to sneak onto his farm to see how he grows wasabi. He now keeps the location of his wasabi farm a closely guarded secret.

23.1   Creating parallel words or phrases

Complete the following sentences, using parallel words or phrases
in each case. (See *The Everyday Writer,* pp. 191–194.) Example:

The wise politician _promises the possible_ , _effects the unavoidable_ ,

and _accepts the inevitable_ .

1. My favorite pastimes include _____ , _____ ,

   and _____ .

2. I want not only _____ but also _____ .

3. My motto is _____ , _____ , and

   _____ .

4. I told my younger sister _____ and

   _____ .

5. _____ , _____ , and _____

   are activities my grandparents enjoy.

6. When he got his promotion, he _____ , _____ ,

   and _____ .

7. You should _____ , _____ , or

   _____ before you invite six guests for dinner.

8. We must either _____ or _____ .

9. Graduates find that the job market _____ ,

   _____ , and _____ .

10. The contract required the workers _____ and

    _____ .

23.2   Revising sentences for parallelism

Revise the following sentences to eliminate any errors in parallel structure. (See *The Everyday Writer*, pp. 191–194.) Example:

> **Pérez Prado's orchestra was famous for playing irresistible rhythms**
>   turning
> **and ~~because it turned~~ the mambo into a new dance craze.**
>   ^

1. The latest dance steps and wearing festive party clothes were necessities for many teenagers in the 1950s.

2. Many people in this country remember how they danced to the mambo music of the 1950s and listening to that era's Latin bands.

3. Older dancers may recall Rosemary Clooney, Perry Como, and Ruth Brown singing mambo numbers and Pérez Prado's band had a huge hit, "Cherry Pink and Apple Blossom White."

4. Growing up near Havana and a student of classical piano, Pérez Prado loved Cuban music.

5. Pérez Prado wanted not only to play Cuban music but also he wanted to combine it with elements of jazz.

6. Playing piano in Havana nightclubs, arranging music for a Latin big band, and the jam sessions he joined with the band's guitarists gave him the idea for a new kind of music.

7. The result was a new dance phenomenon: mambo music was born, and Pérez Prado, who became known as "King of the Mambo."

8. Prado conducted his orchestra with hand-waving, head and shoulder movements, and by kicking his feet high in the air.

9. His recordings feature syncopated percussion, wailing trumpets, and Prado shouted rhythmically.

10. Pérez Prado, innovative and a great musician, died in 1989.

23.3 Revising for parallelism and supplying necessary words

Revise the following paragraph to maintain parallelism where it exists and to supply all words necessary for clarity, grammar, and idiom in parallel structures. (See *The Everyday Writer*, pp. 191–194.)

Family gatherings for events like weddings, holidays, and going on vacation are supposed to be happy occasions, but for many people, getting together with family members causes tremendous stress. Everyone hopes to share warm memories and for a picture-perfect family event. Unfortunately, the reality may include an uncle who makes offensive remarks, a critical mother, or anger at a spouse who doesn't lift a finger to help. Neither difficult relatives nor when things go wrong will necessarily ruin a big family gathering, however. The trick is to plan for problems and being able to adapt. Family members who are not flexible, not pleasant to be around, or willing to do their part may always be a problem for their relatives. However, people who try to make a family gathering a success will almost always either be able to enjoy the event or laugh about it later.

24.1 Revising for verb tense and mood

Revise any of the following sentences in which you find unnecessary shifts in verb tense or in mood. If a sentence is correct as written, write C. (See *The Everyday Writer*, pp. 194–195.) Examples:

The doctor examined six patients, but she only ~~washes~~ washed her hands four times.

Scrub with soap for ten to fifteen seconds and ~~you should~~ rinse thoroughly.

1. Over 150 years ago, a Hungarian doctor discovered that doctors who deliver babies and did not thoroughly wash their hands often spread a deadly infection to new mothers.

2. Today, we know better. It is common knowledge that unclean hands transmit germs.

3. Most people learn as children that keeping their hands clean is very important. However, sometimes they forgot this lesson in later life.

4. All health care workers should know that they had to keep their hands clean.

5. Unfortunately, a new study indicates that a high percentage of busy health care workers did not wash their hands often enough.

6. Hand-washing can be repetitive, time consuming, and boring, but it should be crucial to patient safety in every hospital.

7. Approximately 5 percent of the patients who were admitted to hospitals this year will get an infection there. Some of those infections may be deadly.

8. The bacteria that cause these infections could not travel through the air. They require physical contact to move from place to place.

9. If all hospital workers were to wash their hands regularly, fewer infections travel from patient to patient.

10. Wash your hands frequently, and you should follow these instructions even if your skin gets dry.

24.2 Eliminating shifts in voice and point of view

Revise each of the following sentences to eliminate an unnecessary shift in voice or point of view. (See *The Everyday Writer*, pp. 195–196.) Examples:

                              fiddler played a

The dancers performed on a low stage as a jig ~~was played by a~~

~~fiddler.~~

1. If one visits the local art museum, you will find on display recent prints by Greg Pfarr.

2. I liked the sense of individualism, the crowd yelling for you, and the feeling that I was in command.

3. The police sent protesters to a distant "free speech zone," but supporters were allowed to stand along the motorcade route.

4. When someone says "roommate" to a high school senior bound for college, thoughts of no privacy and potential fights are conjured up.

5. The physician moves the knee around to observe the connections of the cartilage and ligaments, and a fluid is injected into the joint.

6. We knew that you shouldn't walk across the railroad trestle, but we went ahead anyway.

7. When the snapping turtle attacked me and Jake, Jake was bitten on the hand, but I swam away.

8. The roses were gathered by Lionel, and then he arranged them.

9. Sea anemones thrive in coastal tide pools, but it cannot survive outside the water for very long.

10. Suddenly we heard an explosion of wings off to our right, and you could see a hundred or more ducks lifting off from the water.

24.3 Eliminating shifts between direct and indirect discourse

To eliminate the shifts between direct and indirect discourse in the following sentences, put the direct discourse into indirect form. (See *The Everyday Writer,* p. 196.) Example:

> states   his
> Steven Pinker ~~stated~~ that ~~my~~ book is meant for people who use
> language and respect it.

1. Richard Rodriguez acknowledges that intimacy was not created by a language; "it is created by intimates."

2. She said that during a semester abroad, "I really missed all my friends."

3. The bewildered neighbor asked him, "What the heck he thought he was doing on the roof?"

4. Loren Eiseley feels an urge to join the birds in their soundless flight, but in the end he knows that he cannot, and "I was, after all, only a man."

5. The instructor told us, "Please read the next two stories before the next class" and that she might give us a quiz on them.

24.4 Eliminating shifts in tone and diction

Revise each of the following sentences to eliminate shifts in tone and diction. (See *The Everyday Writer*, pp. 196–197.) Example:

How do I
Excuse me. ~~In which direction should I proceed to~~ get to the mall?

1. I am astounded by the number of emails I receive each day trying to flog meds to me.

2. The Chinese invented noodles, even though lots of people think that the Italians must have come up with that bright idea.

3. Most commuters keep to a predictable schedule, hopping a bus or train to the 'burbs at the same time each night.

4. The Guggenheim exhibit of African works of art, often misunderstood and undervalued by Western art historians, is a heck of a show.

5. After she had yanked little William out of the busy street by the strap of his overalls, she tendered a verbal rebuke that left both the child and his mother sniffling.

25.1 Emphasizing main ideas

Revise each of the following sentences to highlight what you take to be the main or most important ideas. (See *The Everyday Writer*, pp. 197–199.) Example:

> **Theories about dinosaurs run the gamut—simple lizards, fully adapted warmblooded creatures, hybrids of coldblooded capabilities,**

1. Also notable is the image of chrysanthemums throughout the story.

2. Although so-called mad cow disease is extremely rare, it eats holes in the brain tissue, depriving its victims of intellect, memory, and life, so people fear it.

3. The case baffled inspectors—even though they found the killer eventually—because of the bizarre nature of the clues and the fact that no one ever heard a thing.

4. A crowd gathered, the stranded whale wriggled off the sandy beach, and a chorus of seagulls cried shrilly.

5. The blogger known only as Atrios writes political commentary successfully enough to attract loyal readers, at least one lawsuit, and plenty of advertisers.

6. Victorian women were warned that if they smoked, they would become sterile, grow a mustache, die young, or contract tuberculosis.

7. All medical papers, whether initial investigation, presentation of final statistics, or reports on work in progress, must undergo rigorous scrutiny.

8. Coast Guard personnel conduct boating safety classes, sometimes must risk their own lives to save others, and monitor emergency radio channels.

9. Since leaving the Pogues, Shane MacGowan has gotten at least as much attention for his excessive drinking as for his music, but he has also recorded albums and toured with a new group.

10. Dr. Carver has separated several pairs of conjoined twins, he grew up in an impoverished family, and he achieved his dream of becoming a surgeon.

26.1 Eliminating unnecessary words and phrases

Make each of the following sentences clear and concise by eliminating unnecessary words and phrases and by making additions or revisions as needed. (See *The Everyday Writer*, pp. 200–203.) Example:

> The ~~incredible, unbelievable~~ feats that Houdini performed amazed ~~and astounded~~ all of his audiences ~~who came to see him.~~

1. Harry Houdini, whose real birth name was Ehrich Weiss, made the claim that he had been born in Appleton, Wisconsin, but in actual fact he was born into the world in Budapest, Hungary.

2. Shortly after Houdini's birth, his family moved to Appleton, where his father served as the one and only rabbi in Appleton at that point in time.

3. Houdini gained fame as a really great master escape artist.

4. His many numerous escapes included getting out of a giant sealed envelope without tearing it and walking out of jail cells that were said to be supposedly escape-proof.

5. Before his untimely early death, Houdini told his brother to burn and destroy all papers describing how Houdini's illusions worked.

6. Clearly, it is quite obvious that Houdini did not want anyone at all to know his hidden secrets.

7. Part of the explanation for Houdini's escape artistry lies in the fact that his physique was in absolutely peak physical condition.

8. Houdini's tremendous control over almost every single individual muscle allowed him to contort his body into seemingly impossible positions.

9. After his mother's death, Houdini grew interested in spiritualism until he discovered that the mediums who were the people running the séances were frauds trying to do nothing more than bilk and cheat their customers.

10. On his deathbed, Houdini promised his wife that he would try and attempt to make contact with her from beyond the grave, but so far, he has never been able to get in touch yet.

26.2 Revising for conciseness

Revise the following paragraph so that each sentence is as concise as possible. Combine or divide sentences if necessary. (See *The Everyday Writer*, pp. 200–203.)

At the present time, one of the most serious problems that faces Americans in the area of public policy is the increasing rise in the cost of health care, which has occurred over an extended period of time. One major aspect of the severe crisis in health care costs is that more and more expensive medical technology is being developed and marketed to doctors and hospitals. Even hospitals that are small in size want the latest kind of diagnostic device. The high cost of this expensive equipment is passed on to consumers, who are the patients. It is then passed on to insurance companies. Therefore, many employers are charging their employees more for health insurance because they themselves are having to pay higher and higher premiums. Others are reducing the employees' coverage to a significant extent. Meanwhile, almost forty million Americans suffer from the condition of a lack of any health insurance. In the event that they have an illness or an injury, they must go to a hospital emergency room. In large cities, emergency rooms are being overwhelmed by people seeking treatment for everything from life-threatening gunshot wounds to broken bones.

27.1   Varying sentence length and structure

The following paragraph can be improved by varying sentence length. Read it aloud to get a sense of how it sounds. Then revise it, creating some short sentences and combining other sentences to create more effective long sentences. Feel free to add words or change punctuation. (See *The Everyday Writer*, pp. 203–206.)

One way to determine whether a car is a good value is for a consumer to find out if it will be expensive to maintain, for a car that needs frequent repairs will cost more than a car that does not. Prospective buyers can get statistics detailing the number of repairs needed for various makes and models of cars, and that information can be useful. But the number of repairs alone does not tell the whole story about the overall cost of a car's maintenance, as foreign cars may cost more to repair than domestic cars. Routine maintenance such as oil changes can cost more on an import, and parts that have to be ordered from distant places can be quite expensive. A buyer may know the number and cost of repairs of a particular car, yet he or she may still encounter surprises. Sometimes a car that is not an especially reliable model may run for thousands of miles with very little maintenance, and the owner will be delighted. The converse is also true, and sometimes a car from a company with an excellent reputation may be in the shop more than on the road. Consumers are better off doing their homework than trusting to instinct when buying a car, but luck will still play a role.

Sentence Grammar

28.1 Identifying subjects and predicates

The following sentences are taken from "A Hanging" and "Shooting an Elephant," two essays by George Orwell. Identify the complete subject and the complete predicate in each sentence, underlining the subject once and the predicate twice. (See *The Everyday Writer*, pp. 218–222.) Example:

> They <u>were going to have their bit of fun after all.</u>

1. His mouth slobbered.

2. It was an immense crowd, two thousand at the least and growing every minute.

3. One could have imagined him thousands of years old.

4. In a job like that, you see the dirty work of Empire at close quarters.

5. All this was perplexing and upsetting.

6. The hangman, a gray-haired convict in the white uniform of the prison, was waiting beside his machine.

7. The dog answered the sound with a whine.

8. Would I please come and do something about it?

9. And at that distance, peacefully eating, the elephant looked no more dangerous than a cow.

10. We set out for the gallows.

28.2 Identifying verbs and verb phrases

Underline each verb or verb phrase in the following sentences. (See *The Everyday Writer*, pp. 220–224.) Example:

> **Many cultures <u>celebrate</u> the arrival of spring with a festival of some kind.**

1. The spring festival of Holi occurs in northern India every March during the full moon.

2. Holi is known as the festival of colors, not only because spring brings flowers, but also because Holi celebrations always include brightly colored dyes.

3. According to legend, the festival of colors began thousands of years ago when Krishna played pranks on girls in his village and threw water on them.

4. During Holi, people toss fistfuls of powdered dyes or dye-filled water balloons at each other and sing traditional Holi songs.

5. Holi festivals allow people freedoms that would be unthinkable during the rest of the year.

6. Any person who is walking outside during a Holi celebration will soon be wearing colored powders or colored water.

7. Men, women, and children can throw powders or dye-filled balloons at anyone, even if the person is much older or of much higher status than they are.

8. Most people wear white clothing for Holi.

9. By the end of the celebration, the white clothes are a riot of color.

10. Doesn't Holi sound like fun?

28.3 Identifying nouns and articles

Identify the nouns, including possessive forms, and the articles in each of the following sentences. Underline the nouns once and the articles twice. (See *The Everyday Writer*, pp. 212, 214.) Example:

The <u>Puritans' hopes</u> were dashed when <u>Charles II</u> regained his father's throne.

1. The squirrel in the front yard seems to have a rat's tail.

2. Alice, please tell me your secret.

3. I washed that mug already.

4. I chose broccoli over asparagus.

5. Henderson's story is a tale of theft and violation.

6. Marlys was startled by her own reflection in the big window.

7. Although plagiarism is dishonest and illegal, it does occur.

8. Nightlife begins in Georgetown even before the sun goes down.

9. In the front row sat two people, a man with slightly graying hair and a young woman in jeans.

10. Journalists should protect their sources except in a serious case in which national security has been compromised.

28.4 Identifying pronouns and antecedents

Identify the pronouns and any antecedents in each of the following sentences, underlining the pronouns once and any antecedents twice. (See *The Everyday Writer*, pp. 212–214.) Example:

A guide <u>dog</u> must handle <u>itself</u> well in any situation.

1. Everyone has seen a guide dog at some time in his or her life.

2. Guide dogs that work with the blind must act as their human partners' eyes.

3. These dogs learn socialization and basic obedience training when they are puppies.

4. Knowing they will have to give up their dog one day, sighted volunteers agree to live with and train a puppy for the first year of its life.

5. Puppies that are destined to be guide dogs are allowed to go into places that routinely refuse entry to other kinds of dogs.

6. If you see a puppy in a supermarket or an office, look for its special coat that identifies it as a trainee guide dog.

7. Volunteer trainers miss their pups after the training period ends, but nothing is more rewarding than knowing that the pups will make life easier for their new owners.

8. Some of the pups do not pass the requirements to become guide dogs, but these are in great demand as household pets.

9. When a dog passes the test and graduates, it and its blind companion learn to work with each other during an intensive training session.

10. If you are interested in learning about guide dogs or in becoming a volunteer, contact your local school for the blind.

28.5 Identifying adjectives and adverbs

Identify the adjectives and adverbs in each of the following sentences, underlining the adjectives once and the adverbs twice. Remember that articles and some pronouns can function as adjectives. (See *The Everyday Writer,* pp. 214–215.) Example:

Underlined in his increasingly tight jeans, he rejected a second

dessert.

1. Politicians must seriously consider how well their lives will withstand intense public scrutiny.

2. Time passed agonizingly slowly, but midnight finally arrived.

3. The shoes in that store are lovely, uncomfortably narrow, and much too expensive.

4. The somewhat shy author spoke reluctantly to six exuberant admirers.

5. I do not want any more of your sorry excuses.

6. The youngest dancer in the troupe performed a brilliant solo.

7. The most instructive of the books is, unfortunately, the longest.

8. Never before has one politician made a bigger mess in this amount of time.

9. Late in the day, the temperature dropped precipitously.

10. Imminent starvation threatens many populations constantly.

28.6 Adding adjectives and adverbs

Expand each of the following sentences by adding appropriate adjectives and adverbs. Delete *the* if need be. (See *The Everyday Writer*, pp. 214–215.) Example:

> Then three   thoroughly   nervous
> The veterinarians examined the patient.
> ^   ^   ^   ^

1. Our assignment is due Wednesday.

2. Most of us enjoy movies.

3. Her superiors praised her work for the Environmental Protection Agency.

4. A corporation can fire workers.

5. The heroine marries the prince.

6. The boardwalk crosses the beach.

7. I have neglected my friend.

8. The media are ignoring his candidacy.

9. Nobody saw the bear, but the ranger said it was dangerous.

10. Which way did you say the pair went?

28.7 Identifying prepositions

Underline the prepositions in the following sentences. (See *The Everyday Writer,* pp. 215–216.) Example:

> Every year, a larger percentage <u>of</u> the population <u>in</u> this country is
>
> <u>over</u> age sixty-five.

1. In the United States, most people prefer not to think about getting older.

2. Popular shows on television delve into the lives of high school and college students, not retirees.

3. Many older Americans complain about feeling invisible in this country, where youth and energy are prized instead of age and experience.

4. Some young people here have very little exposure to their elders and may grow up without knowing their grandparents well.

5. Because many Americans often spend very little time with older people before they are old themselves, some young people see older Americans almost as members of an alien culture.

6. In fact, the only absolute difference between the young and the old is that the elderly have experienced old age in addition to youth.

7. Many people don't think much about the problems of the elderly until middle age, when they may begin to realize what lies ahead of them.

8. Americans in general are living longer lives because of improvements in medical science, and increasing numbers of us are living beyond the age of one hundred.

9. According to most experts, the average age of Americans will continue to rise.

10. Old age does not have to bring an end to mental alertness or physical fitness, and it should not mean isolation from society.

28.8 Identifying conjunctions

Underline the coordinating, correlative, and subordinating conjunctions as well as the conjunctive adverbs in each of the following sentences. Draw a connecting line to show both parts of any correlative conjunctions. (See *The Everyday Writer*, pp. 216–217.) Example:

We used sleeping bags <u>even though</u> the cabin had <u>both</u> sheets <u>and</u> blankets.

1. The shops along the waterfront were open, but business was slow.

2. The colt walked calmly, for he seemed to know he would win the race.

3. Pokey is an outside cat; nevertheless, she greets me at the front door each night as I arrive home.

4. When we arrived at the pond, we saw many children playing there.

5. Either the computer crashed or the power went off; anyway, most of the paper has disappeared.

6. Although I live in a big city, my neighborhood has enough trees and raccoons to make me feel as though I live in the suburbs.

7. Exhausted men and women worked the pumps until their arms ached.

8. I did not know whether to laugh or cry after I realized my mistake.

9. His smug attitude was irritating not only to his administrative assistant but also to the rest of the staff.

10. Because the downtown area has many successful businesses, people still want to live inside the city limits.

28.9 Identifying conjunctions and interjections

Underline conjunctions once and interjections twice in each of the following sentences. Write COORD (for coordinating), CORREL (for correlative), or SUBORD (for subordinating) in parentheses after each sentence to indicate the types of conjunctions in use. (See *The Everyday Writer*, pp. 216–217.) Example:

> <u>Whoops</u>—<u>when</u> I dropped your teacup, it broke. (subord)

1. Dee is arranging her schedule so that she can chair next week's meeting.

2. Hey! Sally took my doll, and I want it back!

3. Jake and Sandy, Elly and Hank, and Sally Jo and Michael all plan to travel together and attend the conference.

4. Um . . . if he isn't here, he must have gone to the store.

5. Before you order dessert, make sure you have enough money to cover it.

6. Until I saw that movie, I never thought about daily life at that time.

7. The rain kept me from mowing the lawn, but I didn't really mind.

8. You performed last night and still passed the test? Wow!

9. If you save money, you'll feel better both now and later.

10. Our parts shipment did not arrive yesterday, so I cannot fill your order.

28.10   Identifying the parts of speech

For each underlined word in the following sentences, write its part of speech as it is used in the sentence. (See *The Everyday Writer*, pp. 211–218.) Example:

> NOUN   ADJ (PROPER)   ADJ
> <u>**Selling**</u> is as <u>**American**</u> as <u>**apple**</u> pie.

1. <u>Advertisements</u> clearly <u>and</u> directly reflect our sense of what we want.

2. Almost every advertisement, whether it <u>is selling</u> beer or <u>cosmetics</u>, implies that we choose certain products because we want to feel more <u>attractive</u>.

3. And as the <u>frequency</u> of <u>movie</u> ads and music ads <u>suggests</u>, we <u>also</u> crave diversion: we want entertainment and relief <u>from</u> stress.

4. We can pretend that we live in <u>Middle Earth</u> for a few hours <u>while</u> we watch *The Lord of the Rings* <u>on</u> DVD.

5. <u>And</u> we can appreciate the verbal wit of Eminem even though most of us have <u>not</u> grown up in a <u>Detroit</u> trailer park.

6. <u>In</u> addition, advertisements suggest <u>that</u> we <u>consistently</u> worry about <u>our</u> health.

7. We are <u>frequently</u> instructed to ask <u>our</u> doctors about new pharmaceutical products, whether or not <u>we</u> need them or understand what they <u>do</u>.

8. We <u>also</u> get appeals to <u>safety</u>, such as ads for giant SUVs <u>that</u> supposedly protect drivers from bad weather and allow them to drive up mountainsides.

9. <u>Naturally</u>, the <u>SUV</u> ads don't reveal that we rarely drive them <u>to</u> destinations more <u>exotic</u> than the supermarket.

10. But <u>hey</u>, if we <u>bought</u> only products we really needed and could afford, <u>who</u> knows what would happen to <u>the</u> American economy?

28.11   Identifying subjects

Identify the complete subject and the simple subject in each sentence. Underline the complete subject once and the simple subject twice. (See *The Everyday Writer*, pp. 219–220.) Example:

> <u>**<u>Telling</u> the absolute truth in a film**</u> **may not be the best way to present a coherent narrative.**

1. The film versions of true stories can play fast and loose with historical facts.

2. Working to "improve" inconvenient or unpoetic facts, writers sometimes try to make a story clearer.

3. Two or more real-life characters may be combined into one fictional character to streamline the script.

4. Because reality seldom has neat beginnings and endings, writers telling a true story may take liberties with the material.

5. The believability of film makes this kind of alteration dangerous.

6. Today's filmmakers have the technological ability to make fiction appear extremely realistic.

7. Viewers without knowledge of the facts may believe that the movie tells the whole truth.

8. Of course, Shakespeare, whose works have recently proved to be a big box-office draw, also revised the facts of history when he wrote plays.

9. However, Shakespeare's seventeenth-century audiences were not likely to forget that they were watching a dramatization.

10. Nobody in the crowd in a Shakespearean theater believed that historical characters spoke in poetry.

28.12 Identifying predicates

Underline the predicate in the following sentences. Then label each verb as linking, transitive, or intransitive. Finally, label all subject and object complements and all direct and indirect objects. (See *The Everyday Writer*, pp. 220–222.) Example:

$$\overline{\text{TV}}\quad\overline{\text{DO}}$$

The governor of Illinois <u>declared</u> <u>a moratorium on executions in his</u>
<u>state</u> in 2000.

1. There were fourteen offenses punishable by death in colonial America.

2. In the 1930s, most Americans still favored capital punishment.

3. However, by the late 1960s, many people in this country found capital punishment unfair and ineffective.

4. Supreme Court justices called capital punishment "cruel and unusual" when they outlawed it in 1972.

5. Most of the justices rejected the method rather than the idea of execution itself.

6. Then, lethal injection was developed as an alternative to older execution methods such as hanging.

7. Support for capital punishment increased dramatically in the 1980s and 1990s with the rising fear of crime.

8. In the past few years, DNA evidence has given more than a hundred prisoners on death row their freedom.

9. Many Americans consider the executions of a few innocent people an acceptable price for capital punishment.

10. In 2004, the United States and China were the only industrialized nations that still used the death penalty.

28.13 Identifying prepositional phrases

Following are some sentences written by the sports columnist Red Smith. Identify and underline all the prepositional phrases. Then choose two of the sentences, and for each, write a sentence that imitates its structure. (See *The Everyday Writer,* p. 223.) Example:

> He glanced <u>about the room</u> <u>with a cocky, crooked grin.</u>
>
> ˙The cat stalked around the yard in her quiet, arrogant way.

1. Fear wasn't in his vocabulary and pain had no meaning.

2. Coaching in Columbus is not quite like coaching in New Haven.

3. He stepped out of the dugout and faced the multitude, two fists and one cap uplifted.

4. The old champ looked fit, square of shoulder and springy of tread, his skin clear, his eyes bright behind the glittering glasses.

5. In those days the Yankees always won the pennant.

28.14 Using prepositional phrases

Combine each of the following pairs of sentences into one sentence by using one or more prepositional phrases. (See *The Everyday Writer,* p. 223.) Example:

> with
> **Teflon is a slippery material. It has many industrial and household uses.**

1. Teflon was invented in 1938. The inventor was Dr. Roy J. Plunkett.

2. Polytetrafluoroethylene (PTFE) is the chemical name. Teflon is the brand name.

3. The benefits of PTFE were immediately obvious. Many scientists understood them.

4. The substance allows food to cook in a pan. The food does not stick.

5. Teflon is not supposed to stick to anything. There is one exception, the pan.

6. Early nonstick cookware coating tended to peel off the surface of the pan. The slightest touch of a metal utensil could remove it.

7. The surface of cookware must be roughened. Then a PTFE primer is applied.

8. The primer holds the PTFE coat in place. A physical bond, not a chemical one, keeps the PTFE on the pan.

9. This slippery substance has kitchen uses. It also protects fabrics from stains.

10. The word *Teflon* can be an adjective. It describes a person who seems to get out of sticky situations easily.

28.15 Identifying verbal phrases

Identify and name each participial phrase, gerund phrase, and infinitive phrase in the following sentences. Identify any sentence in which the verbal phrase acts as the subject of the sentence. (See *The Everyday Writer*, p. 223.) Example:

```
┌──────────────── SUBJECT ────────────────┐
Inventing a computer that can carry on a conversation is not easy.
└GERUND┘
```

1. The brilliant mathematician Alan Turing predicted fifty years ago that people in the year 2000 would have a hard time distinguishing computer chat from human conversation.

2. To check Turing's hypothesis, the annual Loebner competition tests computer programs to determine if any of them can successfully mimic a human conversation.

3. The programs competing for the Loebner prize are called "chatterbots."

4. Programmed for artificial intelligence, the chatterbots are supposed to imitate humans in Internet chat rooms.

5. During the test, human judges trying to tell the machines from human decoys carry on conversations at computer keyboards.

6. Teaching a machine artificial intelligence is extremely difficult.

7. So far, no computer program has managed to win the $100,000 prize.

8. Receiving a $2000 consolation prize was the best that any program in the competition has been able to do.

9. Most of the computer programs in the competition gave themselves away by using either too much logic or too much gibberish.

10. Surprisingly, every human decoy in the competition has also been accused of being a computer by at least one judge.

28.16   **Identifying prepositional, verbal, absolute, and appositive phrases**

Read the following sentences, and identify and label all the prepositional, verbal, absolute, and appositive phrases. Notice that one kind of phrase may appear within another kind. (See *The Everyday Writer*, pp. 223–224.) Example:

```
┌──────── ABSOLUTE ─────────┐          ┌── PREP ──┐
His voice breaking with emotion, Ed thanked us for the award.
              └── PREP ──┘
        └ VERBAL ─────────────┘
```

1. To listen to Patsy Cline is sheer delight.

2. The figure outlined against the sky seemed unable to move.

3. Their tails wagging furiously, the dogs at the shelter worked to win new homes.

4. Jane stood still, her fingers clutching the fence.

5. The moviegoers hissed as the villain enticed the child's dog, a Yorkshire terrier, into his car.

6. Floating on my back, I ignored my practice requirements.

7. His favorite form of recreation was taking a nap.

8. Anna, the leader of the group, was reluctant to relinquish any authority.

9. The sun reflected off the magnificent thunderheads, signaling an approaching storm.

10. Shocked into silence, they kept their gaze fixed on the odd creature.

28.17 Adding prepositional, verbal, absolute, and appositive phrases

Use prepositional, participial, infinitive, gerund, absolute, or appositive phrases to expand each of the following sentences. (See *The Everyday Writer*, pp. 223–224.) Example:

In response to a vigorous shake,
The apples dropped from the limb.
  ^

1. The candidates shook hands with the voters.

2. Teresa looked at her mother.

3. The Sunday afternoon dragged.

4. We were uncertain what to do.

5. Tomás had lost almost all his hair.

6. He wondered about the disappearance.

7. Bandini regretted her crime.

8. The letter lay on the desk.

9. They lived in a trailer.

10. Ten hours of sleep exhausted her.

28.18 Using verbal, absolute, and appositive phrases to combine sentences

Use a participial, infinitive, gerund, absolute, or appositive phrase to combine each of the following pairs of sentences into one sentence. (See *The Everyday Writer*, pp. 223–224.) Example:

> His constant complaining
> ~~He complained constantly. This habit~~ irritated his co-workers.
> ^

1. He relied too much on his computer. That dependence was his downfall.

2. She bought a new camera. This purchase lifted her spirits.

3. His bagpipes droned mournfully. The piper woke up everyone in the apartment building.

4. David Klein performed a monologue. He is an actor and comedian.

5. Have you heard about poisonous cone snails? They live in the Philippines.

6. His concentration on his experiments is intense. He blocks out the rest of the world.

7. Our steep road was treacherous last night. It was covered in two inches of ice.

8. The bird is a gray macaw. It allows no one but Julie to come near it.

9. The large American cockroach's other names are Palmetto bug and water bug. It likes moist environments.

10. The protesters were carrying their banners. They headed down the street.

28.19   Identifying dependent clauses

Underline the dependent clauses, and label any subordinating conjunctions and relative pronouns in each of the following sentences. (See *The Everyday Writer*, pp. 224–226.) Example:

REL. PRON.

The Appalachian Trail, <u>which stretches from Georgia to Maine</u>, is

over 2,100 miles long.

1. Hikers who attempt to walk the whole length of the Appalachian Trail have to put their lives on hold for several months.

2. Most of these hikers start in Georgia when spring arrives in the South.

3. Hikers have to carry all essentials with them because most of the trail meanders through forested mountains far from any towns.

4. Although the Appalachian mountain range has relatively low peaks, they are still a formidable barrier for foot travelers.

5. If a hilly trek with a forty-pound backpack does not sound like a vacation to you, you probably should think twice about taking on the Appalachian Trail.

6. Because the Appalachian Trail lies mainly in wilderness, wild animals are abundant.

7. Many hikers enjoy seeing animals in the wild unless they have a frightening encounter with a bear.

8. Bears that have become accustomed to humans may be a threat to hikers.

9. These bears have learned that people on the Appalachian Trail usually carry plenty of food.

10. Before leaving home, hikers should learn how to react to an aggressive bear to minimize the danger.

28.20   Adding dependent clauses

Expand each of the following sentences by adding at least one dependent clause to it. Be prepared to explain how your addition improves the sentence. (See *The Everyday Writer*, pp. 224–226.) Example:

who think they are the center of the universe
Spoiled children can drive even their parents crazy.

1. Working parents may see their children only at the end of the day.

2. Everyone in a family may have high expectations for time together.

3. Children can easily learn how to manipulate their parents.

4. Whining is difficult to listen to and easy to stop with a new toy or an extra video viewing.

5. However, bribing a child to behave better is a flawed technique.

6. Misbehaving children wear out their welcome quickly.

7. Kids should learn that the world does not revolve around their whims.

8. Parents must learn to stick to their own rules.

9. Enforcing rules sometimes worries parents more than it bothers their children.

10. Even if children protest against discipline, they want to know how to behave.

28.21   Distinguishing between phrases and clauses

The following are some sentences from the letters of E. B. White. Read each one carefully, focusing on the phrases and clauses. Underline any dependent clauses once and any phrases twice. Identify each phrase as a prepositional phrase or a verbal phrase. Finally, choose two sentences, and use them as a model for sentences of your own, imitating White's structure phrase for phrase and clause for clause. (See *The Everyday Writer*, pp. 222–226.) Example:

I was born <u>in 1899</u> and expect <u>to live forever</u>, <u>searching for beauty</u> and <u>raising hell</u> <u>in general</u>.

PREPOSITIONAL PHRASES: in 1899, for beauty, in general
VERBAL PHRASES: to live forever, searching for beauty, raising hell
IMITATION SENTENCE: Sarah was hired in May and plans to work all summer, living at home and saving money for law school.

1. Either Macmillan takes Strunk and me in our bare skins, or I want out.

2. I regard the word *hopefully* as beyond recall.

3. Life in a zoo is just the ticket for some animals and birds.

4. I recall the pleasures and satisfactions of encountering a Perelman piece in a magazine.

5. The way to read Thoreau is to enjoy him—his enthusiasms, his acute perception.

6. You can see at a glance that Professor Strunk omitted needless words.

7. A good many of Charlotte's descendants still live in the barn, and when the warm days of spring arrive there will be lots of tiny spiders emerging into the world.

8. When I start a book, I never know what my characters are going to do, and I accept no responsibility for their eccentric behavior.

9. No sensible writer sets out deliberately to develop a style, but all writers do have distinguishing qualities, and they become very evident when you read the words.

10. When I wrote "Death of a Pig," I was simply rendering an account of what actually happened on my place — to my pig, who died, and to me, who tended him in his last hours.

28.22 Classifying sentences grammatically and functionally

Classify each of the following sentences as simple, compound, complex, or compound-complex. In addition, note any sentences that could be classified as declarative, imperative, interrogative, or exclamatory. (See *The Everyday Writer*, pp. 226–227.) Example:

Stop the thief! simple, imperative

1. During your semester abroad, keep in touch with your family and friends by mail, email, telephone, or even Pony Express if necessary.

2. When I first arrived at college, I became confused about where I fit in and who my role models should be.

3. People go on safari to watch wild animals in their natural habitat.

4. The woman who moved into the apartment next door to mine let her band practice in the living room, but I would not have moved if their music had not been so boring.

5. Should he admit his mistake, or should he keep quiet and hope to avoid discovery?

6. The screen door creaked and banged when she ran into the house.

7. Solve your problems yourself.

8. Retail sales declined as consumers cut back on spending, and many small businesses failed.

9. Why do people insist on drinking coffee when tea tastes so much better?

10. Oh, I detest jokes at other people's expense!

29.1 Using irregular verb forms

Complete each of the following sentences by filling in each blank with the past tense or past participle of the verb listed in parentheses. (See *The Everyday Writer,* pp. 230–233.) Example:

Frida Kahlo _____*became*_____ (become) one of Mexico's foremost

painters.

1. Frida Kahlo _____ (grow) up in Mexico City, where she

   _____ (spend) most of her life.

2. She _____ (be) born in 1907, but she often

   _____ (say) that her birth year _____ (be)

   1910.

3. In 1925 a bus accident _____ (leave) Kahlo horribly injured.

4. The accident _____ (break) her spinal column and many

   other bones, so Kahlo _____ (lie) in bed in a body cast for

   months.

5. She had always _____ (be) a spirited young woman, and

   she _____ (take) up painting to avoid boredom while con-

   valescing.

6. Kahlo _____ (meet) the painter Diego Rivera in 1928 and

   _____ (fall) in love; they married the following year.

7. From the beginning, Rivera had _____ (know) that Kahlo's

   work was remarkable, so he encouraged her to paint.

8. Kahlo _____ (keep) working even though she

   _____ (be) in constant pain for the rest of her life.

9. Kahlo usually _____ (choose) to paint self-portraits; schol-

   ars have _____ (begin) to analyze her unflinching vision of

   herself.

10. The fame of Frida Kahlo has _____ (grow) and

    _____ (spread) since her death in 1954.

29.2 Editing verb forms

Where necessary, edit the following sentences to eliminate any inappropriate verb forms. If the verb forms in a sentence are appropriate as printed, write C. (See *The Everyday Writer*, pp. 230–233.)
Example:

> began
> She ~~begin~~ the examination on time.
> ^

1. The tickets costed almost a hundred dollars apiece, so we decided

   not to see the concert.

2. The lake freezed early this year.

3. The band had sang its last song before the fight begun.

4. Please don't make us any dinner; we have already ate.

5. They had felt that tired only once before.

6. Everyone was shaken up by the turbulence, but the plane landed

   safely.

7. We brung baked beans to the potluck dinner.

8. The accountants must have knowed what the CEO was up to when

   he looted the company.

9. By the mid-1970s, New York had almost went bankrupt.

10. Over the years, Martin has become a close friend.

29.3 Distinguishing between *lie* and *lay, sit* and *set, rise* and *raise*

Choose the appropriate verb form in each of the following sentences. (See *The Everyday Writer,* p. 233.) Example:

The boys laid/lay on the couch, hoping for something good on TV.

1. I sat/set back, closed my eyes, and began to meditate.

2. Mrs. Worth struggled to rise/raise herself to her feet when the judge entered the courtroom.

3. In this area, when the temperature rises/raises, the humidity usually declines.

4. The choir rose/raised up and belted out a hymn.

5. Sitting/Setting in the sun too long can lead to skin cancer.

6. The students sat/set their backpacks down beside their desks and stared grimly at the new teacher.

7. He used whatever was lying/laying around the house.

8. As the flag rose/raised, a trumpeter played "Taps."

9. I lay/laid my books down just as the telephone rang.

10. Sometimes she just lies/lays and stares at the ceiling.

29.4 Deciding on verb tenses

Complete each of the following sentences by filling in the blank with an appropriate form of the verb given in parentheses. Because more than one form will sometimes be possible, choose one form and then be prepared to explain the reasons for your choice. (See *The Everyday Writer,* pp. 234–237.) Example:

Many people ___come/came/have come___ (come) to the United States

seeking religious freedom.

The present tense *come* is appropriate if the sentence states a general truth about immigration; the past tense *came* is appropriate if the sentence refers to immigration at a specific time in the past; the present perfect tense *have come* is appropriate if the sentence refers to immigration that either continues today or ended at an unspecified time in the past. Because the sentence does not provide any information about the time frame to which it refers, any of these answers is acceptable.

1. Every American schoolchild _____ (learn) about the first Thanksgiving.

2. It is true that the Puritans _____ (invite) the most important members of the Wampanoag tribe to join them for the three-day feast.

3. Massasoit and his people _____ (help) the Puritan colony survive during the bitter winter of 1620–1621, so the Puritans thanked them with a harvest celebration.

4. The harvest feast _____ (be) not typical of relations among Puritan colonists and northeastern tribes.

5. Scholars today _____ (conclude) that the Wampanoags and the colonists _____ (disagree) about land use, religion, and other important issues.

6. In an attempt to control the tribes, the colonists _____ (interrogate) Wamsutta, Massasoit's son and successor, in 1662; he _____ (die) shortly afterward.

7. Wamsutta's brother Metacom, known as King Philip, _____ (attack) the colonists in 1675, leading to more than a year of the worst bloodshed the colonies _____ (see).

8. Before the late nineteenth century, most representations of Puritans and Native Americans _____ (show) violent confrontations.

9. While the Indian wars _____ (happen) in the West, images of European colonists and native tribes coexisting peacefully were not popular in the United States.

10. The idea of the peaceful dinner _____ (begin) to appeal to Americans in the twentieth century, when cooperation among different ethnic groups _____ (become) a priority.

29.5 Sequencing tenses

Change the italicized word or phrase in each of the following sentences to create the appropriate sequence of tenses. If a sentence reads acceptably, write C. (See *The Everyday Writer*, pp. 237–238.) Example:

<pre>
                  have sent
He needs to <s>send</s> in his application before today.
             ^
</pre>

1. The crew *had dug* the trench before they installed the cable.

2. Until I started knitting again last month, I *have forgotten* how.

3. *Having sung* in the shower, he did not hear the doorbell.

4. After Darius said that he wanted to postpone college, I *am trying* to talk him out of it.

5. Will you tell Grandpa about your wedding plans when he *has visited* us in the summer?

6. They *hoped* to plant their garden by now.

7. You *will have finished* your paper by the time the semester ends.

8. When he was twenty-one, he *wanted to have become* a millionaire by the age of thirty.

9. The news had just begun when our power *goes* out.

10. *Cutting off* all contact with family, he did not know whom to ask for help.

29.6 Converting the voice of a sentence

Convert each sentence from active to passive voice or from passive to active, and note the differences in emphasis these changes make. (See *The Everyday Writer*, p. 238.) Example:

Machiavelli advises the prince to gain the friendship of the people.

The prince is advised by Machiavelli to gain the friendship of the people.

1. The blog "Talking Points Memo" is maintained by Joshua Micah Marshall.

2. Huge pine trees were uprooted by the storm.

3. Have any spiders been seen in the basement lately?

4. The last doughnut in the box was eaten by Jerry just a few minutes ago.

5. The experimental data are analyzed in the next section of this report.

6. For months, the baby kangaroo is protected, fed, and taught how to survive by its mother.

7. An American teenager narrates DBC Pierre's prizewinning novel about a Columbine-like school shooting, *Vernon God Little*.

8. The lawns and rooftops were covered with the first snow of winter.

9. Marianne avoided such things as elevators, subways, and closets.

10. Suddenly, rainfall pounded on the roof over our heads.

29.7 Using subjunctive mood

Revise any of the following sentences that do not use the appropriate subjunctive verb forms required in formal or academic writing. If the verb forms in a sentence are appropriate as printed, write C. (See *The Everyday Writer*, pp. 239–240.) Example:

                                             were
I saw how carefully he moved, as if he ~~was~~ caring for an infant.
                                             ^

1. Even if I was rich, I wouldn't buy those overpriced shoes.

2. The family requested that contributions be made in Gertrude's memory to a Democratic presidential candidate.

3. The lawyer made it seem as if I was a threat to society.

4. Marie would have gone to the Patti Smith show on New Year's Eve if she would have heard about it in advance.

5. I wish I was with you right now.

6. It is necessary that the manager knows how to do any job in the store.

7. Her stepsisters treated Cinderella as though she was a servant.

8. The invisible announcer requested that audience members should not take photographs.

9. The only requirement is that the tense of both clauses makes sense.

10. If more money was available, we would be able to offer more student scholarships.

30.1 Selecting verbs that agree with their subjects

Underline the appropriate verb form in each of the following sentences. (See *The Everyday Writer,* pp. 240–246.) Example:

Experts on every subject is/<u>are</u> easy to find on the Internet.

1. The desire to find information and answers sends/send many people on Internet searches.

2. There is/are many people who are eager to offer advice online.

3. What credentials does/do these so-called experts have?

4. Problems with using the Internet includes/include the difficulty of determining which sources are reliable.

5. Everyone with access to a computer and a modem has/have the ability to send information over the Internet.

6. Some people put up Web pages that offers/offer impressive but inaccurate data.

7. If a delusional science fiction buff and a respected professor of cosmology writes/write about a new comet, the latter will probably provide better research.

8. To some people, everything on the Internet looks/look equally convincing.

9. A slick design and an eye-catching graphic does/do not mean that the information provided on a Web page is accurate.

10. Learning how to navigate the Web and conduct searches does/do not take the place of developing critical thinking skills.

30.2 Making subjects and verbs agree

Revise the following sentences as necessary to establish subject-verb agreement. If a sentence does not require any change, write C. (See *The Everyday Writer,* pp. 240–246.) Example:

has
A new museum displaying O. Winston Link's photographs ~~have~~
                                                              ^
opened in Roanoke, Virginia.

1. Anyone interested in steam locomotives have probably already heard of the photographer O. Winston Link.

2. Imagine that it are the 1950s, and Link is creating his famous photographs.

3. The steam locomotives — the "iron horses" of the nineteenth century — has begun to give way to diesel engines.

4. Only the Norfolk & Western rail line's Appalachian route still use steam engines.

5. Link, a specialist in public relations, is also a commercial photographer and train lover.

6. He and his assistant Thomas Garver sets up nighttime shots of steam locomotives.

7. Days of setup is required for a single flash photo of a train passing by.

8. Many of the photos show scenes that would have been totally in the dark without Link's flashbulbs.

9. Up to sixteen flashbulbs and specialized reflectors illuminates every important detail.

10. Link's fine photographic eye and his ability to imagine how the flash will look allows him to compose each photo in advance in the dark.

11. His book *Steam, Steel, and Stars* include most of his stunning nighttime train photographs.

12. Famous Link photos such as one of a steam engine passing a drive-in movie appear in the book.

13. Today, the photographs of O. Winston Link has a cult following.

14. More than two thousand negatives from the steam locomotive era belongs to the O. Winston Link Museum in Roanoke.

15. Almost everyone who has seen a Link photograph remembers it.

31.1   Using adjectives and adverbs appropriately

Revise each of the following sentences to maintain correct adverb and adjective use. Then, for each adjective and adverb you've revised, point out the word that it modifies. (See *The Everyday Writer*, pp. 246–251.) Example:

> commonly
> Almost every language ~~common~~ uses nonverbal cues that people can
> interpret.

1. Most people understand easy that raised eyebrows indicate surprise.

2. When a man defiant crosses his arms across his chest, you probably do not need to ask what the gesture means.

3. You are sure familiar with the idea that bodily motions are a kind of language, but is the same thing true of nonverbal sounds?

4. If you feel sadly, your friends may express sympathy by saying, "Awww."

5. When food tastes well, diners express their satisfaction by murmuring, "Mmmm!"

6. If you feel relievedly that a long day is finally over, you may say, "Whew!"

7. These nonverbal signals are called "paralanguage," and they are quick becoming an important field of linguistic study.

8. Paralanguage "words" may look oddly on paper.

9. Written words can only partial indicate what paralanguage sounds like.

10. Lucky for linguists today, tape recorders are readily available.

31.2 Using comparative and superlative modifiers appropriately

Revise each of the following sentences to use modifiers correctly, clearly, and effectively. A variety of acceptable answers is possible for each sentence. (See *The Everyday Writer*, pp. 249–251.) Example:

> When Macbeth and Lady Macbeth plot to kill the king, she shows
> herself to be the ~~most~~ *more* ambitious of the two.

1. The Van Gogh painting was the most priceless.

2. Most of the elderly are women because women tend to live longer.

3. My graduation day will be the most happiest day of my life.

4. Minneapolis is the largest of the Twin Cities.

5. Many couples preparing to marry now arrange for a longer engagement.

6. St. Francis made Assisi one of the famousest towns in Italy.

7. Our team sampled Jujubes, Goldberg's Peanut Chews, and Milk Duds, but we disagreed about which candy was easier on our teeth.

8. That trip to the dentist for a root canal was the unpleasantest experience of my life.

9. You could have found a more nicer way to thank your grandmother for the gift.

10. She has the most unique laugh.

32.1 Revising sentences with misplaced modifiers

Revise each of the following sentences by moving any misplaced modifiers so that they clearly modify the words they are intended to. You may have to change grammatical structures for some sentences. (See *The Everyday Writer*, pp. 252–255.) Example:

Elderly people and students live in the neighborhood
full of identical tract houses
surrounding the university/;which is full of identical tract houses.
^   ^

1. Doctors recommend a new test for cancer, which is painless.

2. The tenor captivated the entire audience singing with verve.

3. I went through the process of taxiing and taking off in my mind.

4. The city approximately spent twelve million dollars on the new stadium.

5. Am I the only person who cares about modifiers in sentences that are misplaced?

6. On the day in question, the patient was not normally able to breathe.

7. Refusing to die at the end of the play, the audience stared in amazement at the actor playing Hamlet.

8. The clothes were full of holes that I was giving away.

9. Revolving out of control, the maintenance worker shut down the turbine.

10. A wailing baby was quickly kissed by the candidate with a soggy diaper.

32.2 Revising squinting modifiers, disruptive modifiers, and split infinitives

Revise each of the following sentences by moving disruptive modifiers and split infinitives as well as by repositioning any squinting modifier so that it unambiguously modifies either the word(s) before it or the word(s) after it. You may have to add words to a sentence to revise it adequately. (See *The Everyday Writer*, pp. 253–254.) Example:

The course we hoped would engross us completely bored us.

The course we hoped would completely engross us bored us.
OR
The course we hoped would engross us bored us completely.

1. Airline security personnel asked Ishmael, while he was hurrying to make his connecting flight, to remove his shoes and socks and to open his carry-on bag.

2. He remembered vividly enjoying the sound of Mrs. McIntosh's singing.

3. Bookstores sold, in the first week after publication, fifty thousand copies.

4. The mayor promised after her reelection she would not raise taxes.

5. The exhibit, because of extensive publicity, attracted large audiences.

6. The collector who owned the painting originally planned to leave it to a museum.

7. Doug hoped to perhaps this time succeed in training the cat to stay in one place even when it was not sleeping.

8. Doctors can now restore limbs that have been severed partially to a functioning condition.

9. A new housing development has gone up with six enormous homes on the hill across the road from Mr. Jacoby's farm.

10. The speaker said when he finished he would answer questions.

11. People who swim frequently will improve their physical condition.

12. The compost smelled after a long summer under the blazing sun pretty bad when I turned it.

13. The state commission promised at its final meeting to make its recommendations public.

14. Stella did not want to argue, after a long day at work and an evening class, about who was going to do the dishes.

15. In the next several months, Lynn hopes to despite her busy schedule of entertaining maintain her diet and actually lose weight.

32.3 Revising dangling modifiers

Revise each of the following sentences to correct the dangling modifiers. (See *The Everyday Writer*, pp. 254–255.) Example:

a viewer gets
Watching television news, an impression is given of constant disaster.

1. High ratings are pursued by emphasizing fires and murders.

2. Interviewing grieving relatives, no consideration is shown for their privacy.

3. To provide comic relief, heat waves and blizzards are attributed to the weather forecaster.

4. Chosen for their looks, the newscasters' journalistic credentials are often weak.

5. As a visual medium, complex issues are hard to present in a televised format.

6. Assumed to care about no one except Americans, editorial boards for network news shows reject many international stories.

7. Generally only twenty-two minutes long, not including commercials, viewers have little time to absorb information.

8. Horrified by stories of bloodshed, the low probability of becoming the victim of crime or terrorism goes unrecognized.

9. Increasing fears among viewers, Americans worry about unlikely events such as children being kidnapped by strangers.

10. Not covering less sensational but more common dangers such as reckless driving and diabetes, viewers may not understand what is really likely to hurt them.

11. Long respected as the best source of news, many readers do not notice their newspapers' flaws and biases.

12. Reporting on a national story, many articles focus on speculation about causes instead of on what actually happened.

13. Influenced subtly by reporters' opinions, newspapers may actually change perceptions of truth.

14. Whether listening to talk radio or watching political talk shows on television, distortions and bias are the norm.

15. By not getting the facts needed to make informed decisions, the news media could do a better job.

33.1 Using subjective case pronouns

Replace the underlined noun or nouns in each of the following sentences with the appropriate subjective case pronoun. (See *The Everyday Writer*, pp. 256–257.) Example:

       he
Jack and ~~George~~ visited the new science library.

1. The person who got the highest mark on the test was <u>Susan</u>.

2. Whenever <u>Jerry, David, and Sean</u> went to the beach, the weather was bad.

3. As the sun rose that morning, Melina considered how lucky <u>Melina</u> was to be able to see it.

4. As the cattle crossed the road, <u>the cattle</u> stopped all traffic.

5. Justin, Paolo, and I have a great time whenever <u>Justin, Paolo, and I</u> get together.

6. The library has a collection of Mark Twain's manuscripts, but <u>the manuscripts</u> are not available to the general public.

7. The cars slowed to a stop whenever <u>the cars</u> approached an on-ramp.

8. <u>Tina, Rahul, Fredo, and I</u> stayed up all night watching the complete box set of *The Godfather* on DVD.

9. Fredo decided that <u>Fredo</u> did not like the scene where Michael has his own brother killed.

10. Maya wondered if <u>Maya</u> were smarter than James.

33.2   Using objective case pronouns

Most of the following sentences use pronouns incorrectly. Revise the incorrect sentences so that they contain correct objective case pronouns. If a sentence is correct, write C. (See *The Everyday Writer*, p. 257.) Example:

> me
> **Eventually, the headwaiter told Kim, Stanley, and I̶ that we could be**
>   ^
> **seated.**

1. Which of the twins are you waiting for — Mary or he?

2. The president gave her the highest praise.

3. Which of those books is for myself?

4. When we asked, the seller promised we that the software would work on a Macintosh computer.

5. Though even the idea of hang gliding made herself nervous, she gave it a try.

6. Max told Jackson and him that the cabin was available to they.

7. Cycling thirty miles a day was triathlon training for Bill, Ubijo, and I.

8. Dennis asked her and me to speak to him in the office.

9. Between you and I, that essay doesn't deserve a high grade.

10. We need two volunteers: yourself and Tom.

33.3 Using possessive case pronouns

Insert a possessive pronoun in the blank in each sentence. (See *The Everyday Writer,* pp. 257–258.) Example:

___My___ **girlfriend bought flowers for me on Valentine's Day.**

1. All day long, people in the office asked admiringly, "_____

   flowers are those?"

2. I told them the bouquet was _____ .

3. The arrangement was perfectly complemented by _____

   vase, which my girlfriend had chosen.

4. _____ selection for me was red roses.

5. Every flower has _____ own meaning, according to a

   Victorian tradition.

6. Roses are easy to understand; _____ meaning is "true

   love."

7. My girlfriend knows that roses are my favorite flower;

   _____ are daffodils.

8. I really appreciated _____ going to the trouble and expense

   of buying me flowers.

9. Not only was it Valentine's Day, but she and I were also celebrating the

   anniversary of _____ first date.

10. That's the story of my most romantic moment; now tell me

    _____ .

33.4   Using *who, whoever, whom,* or *whomever*

Insert *who, whoever, whom,* or *whomever* appropriately in the blank in each of the following sentences. (See *The Everyday Writer,* pp. 258–259.) Example:

She is someone _____who_____ will go far.

1. Professor Quinones asked _____ we wanted to collaborate with.

2. _____ the director chooses to play the lead roles will have to put up with the writer's tantrums.

3. _____ shall I say is calling?

4. Soap operas appeal to _____ is interested in intrigue, suspense, joy, pain, grief, romance, fidelity, sex, and violence.

5. The manager promised to reward _____ sold the most cars.

6. _____ will the new tax law benefit most?

7. The plumbers _____ the landlord hired to install the new toilets in the building have botched the job.

8. The only experts _____ they can recommend are the two magicians who trained them.

9. _____ the voters choose faces an almost impossible challenge.

10. The ballroom is available for children's parties or for _____ wants to rent it.

33.5 Using pronouns in compound structures, appositives, elliptical clauses; choosing between *we* and *us* before a noun

Choose the appropriate pronoun from the pair in parentheses in each of the following sentences. (See *The Everyday Writer,* pp. 259–260.) Example:

Of the group, only (she/her) and I finished the race.

1. All the other job applicants were far more experienced than (I/me).

2. Only (he/him) and the two dressmakers knew what his top-secret fall line would be like.

3. When Jessica and (she/her) first met, they despised each other.

4. Samantha sighed, "I love Benicio del Toro. No one could ever be more beautiful than (he/him)."

5. To (we/us) New Englanders, hurricanes are a bigger worry than tornadoes.

6. The post-holiday credit card bills were a rude shock to Gary and (she/her).

7. Tomorrow (we/us) raw recruits will have our first on-the-job test.

8. The relationship between (they/them) and their brother was often strained.

9. You may think that Anita will win Miss Congeniality, but in fact, everyone likes you better than (she/her).

10. Keith Richards scoffed at the words "Sir Mick Jagger," but (he/him) and Mick apparently don't agree about knighthood.

11. Just between you and (I/me), this seminar is a disaster!

12. Staying a week in a lakeside cabin gave (we/us) New Yorkers a much-needed vacation.

13. Lute Johannson always claimed he was the best of (we/us) chili cookers.

14. Jason is younger than (I/me).

15. Seeing (he and I/him and me) dressed up in her best clothes made

    Mom laugh until she saw the lipstick on the rug.

33.6 Maintaining pronoun-antecedent agreement

Revise the following sentences as needed to create pronoun-antecedent agreement and to eliminate the generic *he* and any awkward pronoun references. Some sentences can be revised in more than one way, and two sentences do not require any change. If a sentence is correct as written, write C. (See *The Everyday Writer,* pp. 260–263.) Example:

> **Everyone should make his own decision about having children.**
>
> Everyone should make his or her own decision about having children.
> OR
> All individuals should make their own decision about having children.

1. Someone who chooses not to have any children of his own is often

   known today as "child-free" rather than "childless."

2. A child-free person may feel that people with children see his time as

   less valuable than their own.

3. Corporate culture sometimes offers parents more time off and other

   perks than it provides to non-parents.

4. A child-free employee may feel that they have to subsidize family med-

   ical plans at work for people who have children.

5. Neither parents nor a child-free person has the right to insist that their

   childbearing choice is the only correct one to make.

6. However, a community has to consider the welfare of their children

   because caring for and educating children eventually benefits everyone.

7. Neither an educated citizenry nor a skilled workforce can exist if they are not financed and helped by older generations.

8. Almost no one would be able to afford to have children if they were expected to pay for educating and training their offspring entirely without help.

9. People who feel that they should not have to help pay for quality day care and schools have not thought through their responsibilities and needs as members of society.

10. As writer Barbara Kingsolver once pointed out, even someone without children will probably need the services of a doctor or a mechanic in their old age.

33.7 Clarifying pronoun reference

Revise each of the following sentences to clarify pronoun reference. All the items can be revised in more than one way. If a pronoun refers ambiguously to more than one possible antecedent, revise the sentence to reflect each possible meaning. (See *The Everyday Writer*, pp. 263–264.) Example:

After Jane left, Miranda found her keys.

Miranda found Jane's keys after Jane left.

Miranda found her own keys after Jane left.

1. Quint trusted Smith because she had worked for her before.

2. Not long after the company set up the subsidiary, it went bankrupt.

3. When drug therapy is combined with psychotherapy, the patients relate better to their therapists, are less vulnerable to what disturbs them, and are more responsive to them.

4. When Deyon was reunited with his father, he wept.

5. Bill smilingly announced his promotion to Ed.

6. On the weather forecast, it said to expect snow in the overnight hours.

7. The tragedy of child abuse is that even after the children of abusive parents grow up, they often continue the sad tradition of cruelty.

8. Lear divides his kingdom between the two older daughters, Goneril and Regan, whose extravagant professions of love are more flattering than the simple affection of the youngest daughter, Cordelia. The consequences of this error in judgment soon become apparent, as they . prove neither grateful nor kind to him.

9. Anna smiled at her mother as she opened the birthday gift.

10. The visit to the pyramids was canceled because of recent terrorist attacks on tourists there, which disappointed Kay, who had waited years to see them.

33.8   Revising to clarify pronoun reference

Revise the following paragraph to establish a clear antecedent for every pronoun that needs one. (See *The Everyday Writer,* pp. 263–264.)

In Paul Fussell's essay "My War," he writes about his experience in combat during World War II, which he says still haunts his life. Fussell confesses that he joined the infantry ROTC in 1939 as a way of getting out of gym class, where he would have been forced to expose his "fat and flabby" body to the ridicule of his classmates. However, it proved to be a serious miscalculation. After the United States entered the war in 1941, other male college students were able to join officer training programs in specialized fields that kept them out of combat. If you were already in an ROTC unit associated with the infantry, though, you were trapped in it. That was how Fussell came to be shipped to France as a rifle-platoon leader in 1944. Almost immediately they sent him to the front, where he soon developed pneumonia because of insufficient winter clothing. He spent a month in hospitals; because he did not want to worry his parents, however, he told them it was just the flu. When he returned to the front, he was wounded by a shell that killed his sergeant.

34.1 Revising comma splices and fused sentences

Revise each of the following comma splices or fused sentences by using the method suggested in brackets after the sentence. (See *The Everyday Writer*, pp. 265–270.) Example:

> but
> **Americans think of slavery as a problem of the past, it still exists**
>   ^
> **in some parts of the world.** [Join with a comma and a coordinating
> conjunction.]

1. We tend to think of slavery only in U.S. terms in fact, it began long before the United States existed and still goes on. [Separate into two sentences.]

2. The group Human Rights Watch filed a report on Mauritania, it is a nation in northwest Africa. [Recast as one independent clause.]

3. Slavery has existed in Mauritania for centuries it continues today. [Join with a comma and a coordinating conjunction.]

4. Members of Mauritania's ruling group are called the Beydanes, they are an Arab Berber tribe also known as the White Moors. [Recast as one independent clause.]

5. Another group in Mauritania is known as the Haratin or the Black Moors, they are native West Africans. [Separate into two sentences.]

6. In modern-day Mauritania many of the Haratin are still slaves, they serve the Beydanes. [Join with a semicolon.]

7. The first modern outcry against slavery in Mauritania arose in 1980, protesters objected to the public sale of an enslaved woman. [Recast as an independent and a dependent clause.]

8. Mauritania outlawed slavery in 1981 little has been done to enforce the law. [Join with a comma and a coordinating conjunction.]

9. The law promised slaveholders financial compensation for freeing their slaves however, the language of the law did not explain exactly who would come up with the money. [Join with a semicolon.]

10. Physical force is not usually used to enslave the Haratin, rather, they are held by the force of conditioning. [Separate into two sentences.]

11. In some ways the Mauritanian system is different from slavery in the United States, there are few slave rebellions in Mauritania. [Join with a comma and a coordinating conjunction.]

12. By some estimates 300,000 former slaves still serve their old masters these slaves are psychologically and economically dependent. [Recast as an independent and a dependent clause.]

13. Many Mauritanian slaves live in their own houses, they may work for their former masters in exchange for a home or for food or medical care. [Recast as an independent and a dependent clause.]

14. In addition, there may be as many as 90,000 Haratin still enslaved, some Beydanes have refused to free their slaves unless the government pays compensation. [Join with a semicolon.]

15. Some Mauritanians claim that slavery is not a problem in their country in fact, in 2001, a Mauritanian official told a United Nations committee that slavery had never existed there. [Join with a dash.]

16. Of course, slavery must have existed in Mauritania there would have been no compelling reason to make a decree to abolish it in 1981. [Join with a comma and a coordinating conjunction.]

17. The president of Mauritania insisted in 1997 that discussions of modern slavery were intended only to hurt the country's reputation his comments did not offer much hope for opponents of slavery. [Recast as an independent and a dependent clause.]

18. Both the slaveholding Beydanes and the enslaved Haratin are made up largely of Muslims, some people in Mauritania see resistance to slavery in their country as anti-Muslim. [Join with a comma and a coordinating conjunction.]

19. In some cases, Western opponents of Mauritanian slavery may indeed harbor anti-Muslim sentiments that does not justify allowing the slavery to continue. [Join with a semicolon.]

20. Islamic authorities in Mauritania have agreed that all Muslims are equal therefore, one Muslim must not enslave another. [Join with a semicolon.]

34.2 Revising comma splices

Revise the following paragraph, eliminating all comma splices by using a period or a semicolon. Then revise the paragraph again, this time using any of these three methods:

Separate independent clauses into sentences of their own.

Recast two or more clauses as one independent clause.

Recast one independent clause as a dependent clause.

Comment on the two revisions. What differences in rhythm do you detect? Which version do you prefer, and why? (See *The Everyday Writer*, pp. 265–270.)

My sister Mary decided to paint her house last spring, thus, she had to buy some paint. She wanted inexpensive paint, at the same time, it had to go on easily and cover well, that combination was unrealistic to start with. She had never done exterior painting before, in fact, she did not even own a ladder. She was a complete beginner, on the other hand, she was a hard worker and was willing to learn. She got her husband, Dan, to take a week off from work, likewise she let her two teenage sons take three days off from school to help. Mary went out and bought the "dark green" paint for $6.99 a gallon, it must have been mostly water, in fact, you could almost see through it. Mary and Dan and the boys put one coat of this paint on the house, as a result, their white house turned a streaky light green. Dan and the boys rebelled, declaring they would not work anymore with such cheap paint. Mary was forced to buy all new paint, even so, the house did not really get painted until September.

34.3 Revising comma splices and fused sentences

Revise the following paragraph, eliminating the comma splices and fused sentences by using any of these methods:

Separate independent clauses into sentences of their own.

Link clauses with a comma and a coordinating conjunction.

Link clauses with a semicolon and, perhaps, a conjunctive adverb or a transitional phrase.

Recast two or more clauses as one independent clause.

Recast one independent clause as a dependent clause.

Link clauses with a dash.

Then revise the paragraph again, this time eliminating each comma splice and fused sentence by using a different method. Decide which paragraph is more effective, and why. Finally, compare the revision you prefer with the revisions of several other students, and discuss the ways in which the versions differ in meaning. (See *The Everyday Writer,* pp. 265–270.)

When most Americans think of drug dealers, they picture a shadowy figure in a dark alley, there are illicit drug deals in small-town homes and farmhouses, too. A recent survey of young Americans provided evidence that rural teens are more likely than urban ones to use illegal drugs, the young people's drugs of choice include not only marijuana but also methamphetamine and other substances. Meth labs seem to be appearing in more and more small towns these chemical labs are easy and inexpensive to set up in a home or an outbuilding. Methamphetamine addiction is on the rise in rural America, a fact that is devastating to local communities and shocking to those who live elsewhere. Outsiders are likely to forget that rural America is frequently impoverished the teens in poor rural areas are as likely as urban youth to feel bored and trapped in a dead-end existence. Open country and trees are all very well, if there are no jobs, can young people live on bucolic scenery? Many of these teens have seen their parents struggle they cannot really expect their lives to be significantly different. A rural upbringing can't protect children from drugs ensuring that they have hope and constructive ways to spend their time is a much more effective deterrent.

35.1 Eliminating sentence fragments

Revise each of the following fragments, either by combining fragments with independent clauses or by rewriting them as separate sentences. (See *The Everyday Writer*, pp. 271–274.) Example:

Zoe looked close to tears. Standing with her head bowed.

Standing with her head bowed, Zoe looked close to tears.

Zoe looked close to tears. She was standing with her head bowed.

1. Wollstonecraft believed in universal public education. Also, in education that forms the heart and strengthens the body.

2. Her father pulled strings to get her the job. Later regretting his actions.

3. Organized crime has been able to attract graduates just as big business has. With good pay and the best equipment money can buy.

4. Trying to carry a portfolio, art box, illustration boards, and drawing pads. I must have looked ridiculous.

5. The president promoted one tax change. A reduction in the capital gains tax.

6. Connie picked up the cat and started playing with it. It scratched her neck. With its sharp little claws.

7. The climbers had two choices. To go over a four-hundred-foot cliff or to turn back. They decided to make the attempt.

8. The region has dry, sandy soil. Blown into strange formations by the ever-present wind.

9. The appeal of this film is obvious. Its enthusiastic embrace of sex and violence.

10. To feel useful. Many older Americans want nothing more than that.

35.2   Revising a paragraph to eliminate sentence fragments

Underline every fragment you find in the following paragraph. Then revise the paragraph. You may combine or rearrange sentences as long as you retain the original content. (See *The Everyday Writer*, pp. 271–274.)

It must be embarrassing for famous people. To have people think that they are dead when they aren't. I'm not talking about whispered conspiracies. Like all of those supposed clues on Beatles albums about Paul McCartney's supposed demise. (In case you were wondering. Paul is alive and well and now a knight, no less.) Instead, I'm thinking about half-forgotten celebrities. Actors and musicians who are not among your favorites may get mixed up in your mind. Before you know it. You're saying to a friend, "I thought that guy was dead." Then you may both debate for a while. Because neither of you is certain whether the guy really is dead or whether you're thinking of someone else who sort of resembled him. It's a good thing so many celebrity reality shows and exposés feature the has-beens you barely remember. With those shows. You at least know that the people on screen are still alive. Or if they aren't. They have died recently enough that you will probably still remember.

35.3 Understanding intentional fragments

Choose an advertisement from a newspaper or magazine that contains intentional fragments. Rewrite the advertisement to eliminate all sentence fragments. Be prepared to explain how your version and the original differ in impact and why you think the copywriters for the ad chose to use fragments rather than complete sentences. (See *The Everyday Writer,* pp. 271–274.)

Language/Glossary of Usage

37.1 Identifying stereotypes

Each of the following sentences stereotypes a person or a group of people. Underline the word or phrase that identifies the stereotyped person or group. In each case, be ready to explain why the stereotype may be offensive, demeaning, or unfair. (See *The Everyday Writer*, p. 283.) Example:

> **If you have trouble printing, ask a <u>computer geek</u> for help.**
>
> Assumes that all computer-savvy people are geeky, which is not the case.

1. The comedy show flopped because those rednecks in the audience don't understand satire.

2. Academics are extremely well paid, considering how few hours they actually teach.

3. Only a New Yorker could be so indifferent to the feelings of others.

4. I would never travel to France because everyone there hates Americans.

5. College kids need real-world experience.

6. Dropouts have trouble landing good jobs.

7. When we visit the nursing home, remember to treat each of the old folks with respect.

8. The ambulance chasers have clogged our court system.

37.2 Identifying and revising sexist language

The following excerpt is taken from the 1968 edition of Dr. Benjamin Spock's *Baby and Child Care*. Read it carefully, noting any language we might today consider sexist. Then try bringing it up to date by revising the passage, substituting nonsexist language as necessary. (See *The Everyday Writer*, p. 284.)

399. Feeling his oats. One year old is an exciting age. Your baby is changing in lots of ways—in his eating, in how he gets around, in what he wants to do and in how he feels about himself and other people. When he was little and helpless, you could put him where you wanted him, give him the playthings you thought suitable, feed him the foods you knew were best. Most of the time he was willing to let you be the boss, and took it all in good spirit. It's more complicated now that he is around a year old. He seems to realize that he's not meant to be a baby doll the rest of his life, that he's a human being with ideas and a will of his own.

When you suggest something that doesn't appeal to him, he feels he must assert himself. His nature tells him to. He just says No in words or actions, even about things that he likes to do. The psychologists call it "negativism"; mothers call it "that terrible No stage." But stop and think what would happen to him if he never felt like saying No. He'd become a robot, a mechanical man. You wouldn't be able to resist the temptation to boss him all the time, and he'd stop learning and developing. When he was old enough to go out into the world, to school and later to work, everybody else would take advantage of him, too. He'd never be good for anything.

37.3   Rewriting to eliminate offensive references

Review the following sentences for offensive references or terms. If a sentence seems acceptable as written, write C. If a sentence contains unacceptable terms, rewrite it. (See *The Everyday Writer*, pp. 283–287.) Example:

> Passengers
> ~~Elderly passengers~~ on the cruise ship *Romance Afloat* will enjoy
> ^
> swimming, shuffleboard, and nightly movies.

1. A West Point cadet must keep his record clean if he expects to excel in his chosen career.

2. All of the children in the kindergarten class will ask their mothers to help make cookies for the bake sale.

3. People like mill workers probably don't listen to the classical music station.

4. Acting as a spokesman and speaking with a southern twang, Cynthia McDowell, attractive mother of two, vowed that all elementary school-teachers in the district would take their turns on the picket line until the school board agreed to resume negotiations.

5. If you can find a mechanic today, see if he will be able to look at the car before morning.

6. Seventy-six-year-old Jewish violinist Josh Mickle, last night's featured soloist, brought the crowd to its feet.

7. Our skylight was installed last week by a woman carpenter.

8. Despite the plane's mechanical problems, the crewmen were able to calm the passengers and land safely.

9. Blind psychology professor Dr. Charles Warnath gave the keynote address last night.

10. Catholic attorney Margaret Samuelson won her sixteenth case in a row last week.

38.1 Considering ethnic and regional varieties of English

Read the following examples by authors using ethnic and regional varieties of English. See if you can "translate" each of them into standard academic English. Once you have your translated sentences, write a paragraph (in standard academic English) discussing (1) the differences you detect between standard academic English and the ethnic or regional example, and (2) the effects that are achieved by using each variety of English. (See *The Everyday Writer,* pp. 289, 290.)

"Hey!" squeaked Curtis, his expression amazed. "I got myself shot in the back!"

Beside him, Lyon lifted Curtis' tattered T-shirt, plain and faded black like the other boys' . . . gang colors. "Yeah? Well, you for sure be takin it cool, man. Let's check it out."

. . . Finally, he smiled and parted Curtis' arm. "It be only a cut. Like from a chunk of flyin brick or somethin. Nowhere near his heart. That be all what matter." —Jess Mowry, *Way Past Cool*

". . . You look like you come from here but don't sound it."

"My people came from Quoyle's Point but I was brought up in the States. So I'm an outsider. More or less." Quoyle's hand crept up over his chin.

The harbormaster looked at him. Squinted.

"Yes," said Diddy Shovel. "I guess you got a story there, m'boy. How did it all come about that you was raised so far from home? That you come back?" —E. Annie Proulx, *The Shipping News*

39.1   Using formal register

Revise each of the following sentences to use formal register consistently, eliminating colloquial or slang terms. (See *The Everyday Writer*, pp. 292–295.) Example:

> Although   be excited   as soon as
> I can ~~get all enthused~~ about writing, ~~but~~ I sit down to write my
> ^   ^
>   blank.
> mind goes ~~right to sleep.~~
>   ^

1. James Agee's most famous novel, *A Death in the Family*, focuses on a young boy and on what happens after his old man kicks in a car wreck.

2. The young dancers stamped their feet so that their anklets jingled, and the audience eyeballed them approvingly.

3. This essay will trash Mr. Buckley's wacko argument.

4. We decided not to buy a bigger car that got lousy gas mileage and instead to keep our old Honda.

5. Often, instead of firing an incompetent teacher, school officials will transfer the person to another school in order to avoid the hassles involved in a dismissal.

6. After she had raced to the post office at ten minutes to five, she realized that she had completely spaced the fact that it was a federal holiday.

7. Desdemona's attitude is that of a wimp; she just lies down and dies, accepting her death as inevitable.

8. Moby Dick's humongous size was matched only by Ahab's obsessive desire to wipe him out.

9. My family lived in Trinidad for the first ten years of my life, and we went through a lot; but when we came to America, we thought we had it made.

10. The class misbehaved so dreadfully in their regular teacher's absence

that the substitute lost it.

39.2 Determining levels of language

For each of the scenarios below, note who the audience would be for the piece or writing. Then circle the level of formality that would be appropriate. Be prepared to explain your answer. (See *The Everyday Writer*, pp. 292–295.) Example:

An Internet chat room for people who are interested in Harley-

Davidson motorcycles

Level of formality:

(informal)   **formal**

Audience: _____ *others who share your passion* _____

1. An email to a childhood friend across the country

Level of formality:

informal   formal

Audience: _____

2. A letter requesting an interview in response to a help-wanted advertise-

ment in the newspaper

Level of formality:

informal   formal

Audience: _____

3. A brochure explaining the recycling policies of your community to local

residents

Level of formality:

informal   formal

Audience: _____

4. A letter to the editor of the *Washington Post* explaining that a recent
   editorial failed to consider all the facts about health maintenance
   organizations (HMOs)

   Level of formality:

   informal   formal

   Audience: _____

5. A cover letter asking a professor to accept the late paper you are
   sending after the end of the semester.

   Level of formality:

   informal   formal

   Audience: _____

39.3 Checking for correct denotation

Read each of the following sentences, looking for errors in denota-
tion and using your dictionary as needed. Underline every error that
you find. Then examine each error to determine the word intended,
and write in the correct word. If a sentence has no error, write C. (See
The Everyday Writer, pp. 295–296.) Example:

> adapted
> **Peregrine falcons, once an endangered species, have ~~adopted~~ to**
> ^
> **nesting in cities instead of wilderness areas.**

1. As recently as 1970, many people thought that the distinction of the
   peregrine falcon was inevitable.

2. The falcons' situation reached its apex that year, when there were no wild
   pairs of breeding peregrine falcons anywhere east of the Rocky Mountains.

3. Until 1965, the descent of the falcons was blamed on overdevelopment
   and hunting.

4. The real problem, which effected many other large birds, was the widespread use of the pesticide DDT.

5. Byproducts of the chemical remain for long periods in the body, and the falcons, which are at the top of the food chain, consumed concentrated doses.

6. DDT made the shells of the birds' eggs so brittle that they shattered when the falcons tried to incubate them.

7. The federal government banded the use of DDT, but the falcons needed even more assistance from humans.

8. Thin-shelled falcon eggs were taken from nests and replaced by plaster ones so the parent birds had the delusion that they were incubating eggs.

9. Meanwhile, the eggs were hatched in lavatories, and the chicks were returned to their parents' cliffside nests and raised there.

10. Retrofitting the falcons to the East Coast has been wildly successful, and New York City, with its clifflike skyscrapers, is now home to breeding pairs of peregrines.

39.4 Revising sentences to change connotations

The sentences that follow contain words with strongly judgmental connotative meanings. Underline these words; then revise each sentence to make it more neutral. (See *The Everyday Writer*, pp. 295–296.) Example:

> **The current NRA <u>scheme</u> appeals to patriotism as a <u>smokescreen to obscure the real issue</u> of gun control.**
>
> The current NRA campaign appeals to patriotism rather than responding directly to gun-control proposals.

1. The Democrats are conspiring on a new education bill.

2. CEOs waltz away with millions in salary, stock options, and pensions while the little people who keep the company running get peanuts.

3. Only recently have ladies landed a seat on the Supreme Court.

4. Tree-huggers ranted about the Explorer's gas mileage outside the Ford dealership.

5. Bloodthirsty fans bellowed mindlessly for the referee's head after the call went against the thugs on the home team.

6. Naive voters often stumble to the polls and blithely yank whichever handles are closest to them.

7. Liberals constantly whine about protecting civil rights, but they don't care about protecting the flag that Americans have fought and died for.

8. A mob of protesters appeared, yelling and jabbing their signs in the air.

39.5 Considering connotation

Study the italicized words in each of the following passages, and decide what each word's connotations contribute to your understanding of the passage. Think of a synonym for each word, and see whether you can decide what difference the new word would make to the effect of the passage. (See *The Everyday Writer,* pp. 295–296.) Example:

> It is a story of extended horror. But it isn't only the horror that *numbs* response. Nor is it that the discoverer [Columbus] *deteriorates* so steadily after the discovery. It is the *banality* of the man. He was looking less for America or Asia than for gold; and the banality of expectation matches a continuing banality of *perception.*
>
> –V. S. NAIPAUL, "Columbus and Crusoe"
>
> *numbs:* deadens, paralyzes
> *deteriorates:* declines, gets worse
> *banality:* ordinariness, triviality
> *perception:* understanding, judgment

1. The Burmans were already *racing* past me across the mud. It was obvious that the elephant would never *rise* again, but he was not dead. He was breathing very rhythmically with long *rattling* gasps, his great *mound* of a side painfully rising and falling.
    – GEORGE ORWELL, "Shooting an Elephant"

2. Then one evening Miss Glory told me to serve the ladies on the porch. After I set the tray down and turned toward the kitchen, one of the women asked, "What's your name, *girl*?"
    – MAYA ANGELOU, *I Know Why the Caged Bird Sings*

3. We caught two bass, *hauling* them in *briskly* as though they were mackerel, pulling them over the side of the boat in a *businesslike* manner without any landing net, and stunning them with a *blow* on the back of the head.
    – E. B. WHITE, "Once More to the Lake"

4. The Kiowas are a summer people; they *abide* the cold and keep to themselves; but when the season *turns* and the land becomes warm and *vital*, they cannot *hold still*.
    – N. SCOTT MOMADAY, "The Way to Rainy Mountain"

5. If boxing is a sport, it is the most *tragic* of all sports because, more than any [other] human activity, it *consumes* the very excellence it *displays:* Its very *drama* is this consumption.
    – JOYCE CAROL OATES, "On Boxing"

39.6 Using specific and concrete words

Rewrite each of the following sentences to be more specific and more concrete. (See *The Everyday Writer*, p. 296.) Example:

The weather this summer has varied.

Going from clear, dry days, on which the breeze seems to scrub the sky, to the so-called dog days of oppressive humidity, July and August have offered two extremes of weather.

1. The child played on the beach.

2. He isn't terribly handsome, but he's a lot of fun.

3. The attendant came toward my car.

4. Children sometimes behave badly in public.

5. The entryway of the building was dirty.

6. Robert was not feeling well, so he stayed home from the party.

7. My neighbor is a nuisance.

8. Sunday dinner was good.

9. The sounds at dawn are memorable.

10. Central Texas has an unusual climate.

39.7 Thinking about similes and metaphors

Identify the similes and metaphors in the following numbered items, and decide how each contributes to your understanding of the passage or sentence in which it appears. (See *The Everyday Writer*, p. 297.) Example:

> **The tattoo he had gotten as a teenager, now a blue bruise underneath the word "Mom," remained his favorite souvenir.**
>
> *a blue bruise* (metaphor): makes vivid the tattoo's appearance

1. The fog hangs among the trees like veils of trailing lace.
   – STEPHANIE VAUGHN, "My Mother Breathing Light"

2. The clouds were great mounds of marshmallow fluff heaped just below the wings of the passing airplane.

3. The migraine acted as a circuit breaker, and the fuses have emerged intact.
   – JOAN DIDION, "In Bed"

4. As Serena began to cry, James felt as if someone had punched him in the stomach.

5. Black women are called, in the folklore that so aptly identifies one's status in society, "the mule of the world," because we have been handed the burdens that everyone else—everyone else—refused to carry.
   – ALICE WALKER, *In Search of Our Mothers' Gardens*

6. John's mother, Mom Willie, who wore her Southern background like a magnolia corsage, eternally fresh, was robust and in her sixties.
   – MAYA ANGELOU, "The Heart of a Woman"

7. According to Dr. Seuss, the Grinch is a bad banana with a greasy black peel.

8. I was watching everyone else and didn't see the waitress standing quietly by. Her voice was deep and soft like water moving in a cavern.
   – WILLIAM LEAST HEAT MOON, "In the Land of 'Coke-Cola'"

9. The clicking sounds of the rotary phone were as old-fashioned and charming as the song of a square dance caller.

10. My horse, when he is in his stall or lounging about the pasture, has the same relationship to pain that I have when cuddling up with a good murder mystery—comfort and convenience have top priority.
    – VICKI HEARNE, "Horses in Partnership with Time"

40.1 Recognizing correct spellings

Choose the correct spelling from the pair of words in parentheses in each of the following sentences. (See *The Everyday Writer,* pp. 299–300.) Example:

Today, many small filmmakers have a straight-to-video
(**business**/busyness) plan.

1. The "straight-to-video" strategy was once reserved only for (truely/truly) bad movies that were sure to (loose/lose) money in theaters.

2. Disney and other makers of children's films were the first to (sense/since) that a straight-to-video release could be a hit in stores.

3. A sequel to almost any hit children's movie can use characters and plot points that are (all ready/already) (developed/developped).

4. The audience for such sequels is (apparently/apparantly) unlimited, and children cheerfully (harass/harrass) their parents for multiple versions of *The Lion King* or *The Land before Time*.

5. But independent filmmakers have also (successfully/sucessfully) created unique straight-to-video hits for specialized audiences.

6. Straight-to-video films—(which/witch) today usually go straight to DVD—are often made by young filmmakers who have a hard time getting their films (accepted/excepted) in theaters.

7. For example, many young filmmakers (beleive/believe) that getting their films into stores is the only way to make them available to a potential audience.

8. Films that appear first in stores may or may not be (especially/specially) good, and they have usually cost very little money to make.

9. Spending (a lot/alot) of money on making a movie does not (neccessarily/necessarily) mean that the movie will be good, in any case.

10. Local audiences who (know/no) what they want to see are snapping up films in the store, and filmmakers can make a (profit/prophet)—and perhaps another film.

40.2 Proofreading for spelling

The following paragraph has already been checked using a word processor's spelling checker. Correct any spelling errors that may remain. (See *The Everyday Writer*, pp. 299–300.)

All though many Americans recognize that they need to loose wait, most people are not a ware that there pets may be to fat, to. About 30 percent of the cats an dogs in this country are over weight. According to veterinarians, this is the leading health problem for America's pets. Some times people feed their pets to much out of miss guided love for the animal. In edition, people who are in active are likely to have in active pets that may be prone to obesity. If the owners can not feel they're pet's ribs, the pet needs too go on a diet. Like over wait humans, fat pets are libel to suffer a number of health problems. It is no kindness to an animal too let it eat more then it should.

40.3 Distinguishing among homonyms

Choose the appropriate word in each set of parentheses. (See *The Everyday Writer*, pp. 300–302.) Example:

Antifreeze can have a toxic (affect / <u>effect</u>) on pets.

People need antifreeze in (their/there/they're) cars in cold (weather/whether). Unfortunately, antifreeze also tastes (grate/great) to cats and dogs, who drink it from the greenish puddles commonly (scene/seen) on asphalt. Antifreeze made of ethylene glycol causes kidney failure and has (lead/led) to the deaths of many pets. (Its/It's) not (to/too/two) hard to protect (your/you're) animals from antifreeze poisoning, however. First, (buy/by) antifreeze that does not contain ethylene glycol, in spite of (its/it's) higher cost. Second, do not let pets wander out of (cite/sight/site) when they are outdoors. Third, if a pet acts sick, get help even if the animal (seams/seems) to improve—animals with antifreeze poisoning appear to feel better shortly before they (die/dye). And finally, give the animal vodka or other liquor as an antidote, but only if (their/there/they're) is no way for a veterinarian to look at your pet immediately.

40.4 Spelling plurals

Form the plural of each of the following words. (See *The Everyday Writer*, pp. 303–304.) Example:

fox *foxes*

1. beach   7. rose

2. phenomenon   8. stepchild

3. golf club   9. turkey

4. medium   10. baby

5. radio   11. tomato

6. crutch   12. sergeant-at-arms

41.1 Selecting the appropriate word

Choose the appropriate word for each of the following sentences from the pair of words in parentheses. (See *The Everyday Writer*, pp. 305–313.) Example:

She looked fragile and (<u>weak</u> / week).

1. I burned off (fewer/less) calories than I'd hoped to.

2. If the two of them can't reach an agreement, they're going to have to call in a (disinterested/uninterested) party.

3. We hiked (farther/further) than we had intended.

4. At the press conference, the president did not (allude/elude) to the growing scandal.

5. The (amount/number) of applications for the two minimum-wage jobs astounded Gracie.

6. The (reason/reason why) she didn't win the race should be self-evident.

7. No one (beside/besides) my younger brother wants to go to the circus.

8. When he (raises/rises) his glass in a toast, be polite enough to stand up.

9. Hodges and Smith told (each other/one another) about the questions the arresting officer had asked.

10. Set off the (quotation/quote) with the appropriate punctuation.

11. He feels (bad/badly) that he hurt my feelings.

12. Waving her arm in front of Mary's nose, Rose (flaunted/flouted) her expensive new bracelet.

13. She annoyed the host by not immediately (accepting/excepting) the invitation.

14. Mr. Higgins loudly told his employees to think (outside/outside of) the box, and they all rolled their eyes.

15. We decided to go to the concert, (irregardless/regardless) of the fact that Mom had warned us not to.

16. The three (principals/principles) in the company couldn't agree among themselves.

17. The calm (preceded/proceeded) the storm.

18. The ticket to the concert was considerably more expensive (than/then) I'd hoped it would be.

19. Answer the judge clearly and (respectfully/respectively).

20. Giovanni has to convince himself to go to school (every day/everyday).

41.2 Editing inappropriate words

In each of the following sentences, remove or replace inappropriate words. If all the words in a sentence are appropriate, mark the sentence C. (See *The Everyday Writer*, pp. 305–313.) Example:

> The pilot ~~can't~~ can hardly see in such a fog.

1. I was good and ready for the final exam.

2. When he finally mastered the program, the trainee had a tendency to flaunt his newly acquired talent.

3. When I loose weight, my clothes become loose.

4. Johanna hanged the sheets on the line because the fresh air made them smell good, but the neighbors complained.

5. Every time I go to the supermarket, I get less items for the same amount of money.

6. The supervisor and the trainee speak to each other everyday.

7. The principal could of been more encouraging when talking to the parents.

8. After gathering the chemicals and the instruments, you can proceed with the experiment.

9. Howie tried working out on a stationery bicycle, but he hated pedaling fast and going nowhere.

10. A small percent of the graduates weren't qualified for the entry-level positions.

11. If they are holding out for a consensus of opinion, they are going to have a long wait.

12. Swiss cheese is different than Jarlsberg.

13. The rich cream complements the figs.

14. Maybe we will fly to California to see Uncle Doug in the fall, but we may be too deeply in debt to take a vacation then.

15. Miranda has been working eleven-hour days since she learned that management is planning another round of layoffs.

16. She emigrated to New York in the 1920s.

17. Jackson Pollock created a new affect by dribbling paint on the canvas.

18. My visiting relatives made theirselves look like tourists by wearing white sneakers and by staring at all of the tall buildings.

19. She is literally dying to see that movie.

20. Hopefully, it won't rain during the company outing.

Punctuation/Mechanics

42.1 Using a comma to set off introductory elements

In the following sentences, add any commas that are needed after the introductory element. If no comma is necessary, write C. (See *The Everyday Writer*, pp. 318–319.) Example:

Using technology in new ways, scientists are working on an electronic nose.

1. Although the idea of an electronic nose may sound odd such a nose would have many uses.

2. In the past doctors recognized some ailments by a characteristic odor.

3. Having strep throat causes a person to give off a particular scent that a trained nose can identify.

4. Of course throat cultures can also spot strep throat, but they take time.

5. When a strep infection is identified immediately by its smell a patient can get immediate treatment.

6. Someday electronic noses may be perfected.

7. Along with this technological advance is likely to come disbelief that electronic noses could be useful.

8. Naturally people may appreciate the idea of using electronic noses to avoid invasive medical procedures.

9. But if electronic noses get more sensitive they could be used for tasks human noses find unpleasant.

10. Unable to judge whether smells are delectable or nauseating an electronic nose might be a valuable aid to a human one.

42.2   Using a comma in compound sentences

Use a comma and a coordinating conjunction (*and, but, or, for, nor, so,* or *yet*) to combine each of the following pairs of sentences into one sentence. Delete or rearrange words if necessary. (See *The Everyday Writer,* pp. 319–320.) Example:

The phrase *test-tube baby* is rarely used today. ,yet In vitro fertilization is common.

1. Treatments for infertility become more promising each year. In vitro fertilization has helped many people have children.

2. Over two decades ago, fertility treatments were a little-explored field. The first "test-tube baby" astonished the world.

3. *In vitro* means "in glass." In vitro fertilization does indeed take place in a lab dish.

4. A scientist combines an egg cell and a sperm cell. An embryo forms when the egg cell begins to divide.

5. The embryo that grows is returned to the mother's uterus. The process of growing to viability cannot take place entirely in a laboratory.

6. The procedure requires scientific intervention. The parents of a "test-tube baby" have a child that is biologically theirs.

7. Before in vitro fertilization, would-be parents might have given up on the idea of having children. They might have spent years trying to adopt a child.

8. In vitro fertilization has helped many people have children. It is expensive.

9. There are other, newer methods of helping infertile couples. In vitro fertilization no longer astonishes the public.

10. The first "test-tube baby," who was born in England, was a celebrity. Today, children whose parents used in vitro fertilization are quite common.

42.3 Recognizing restrictive and nonrestrictive elements

First, underline the restrictive or the nonrestrictive elements in the following sentences. Then, use commas to set off the nonrestrictive elements in any of the sentences that contain such elements. (See *The Everyday Writer*, pp. 320–323.) Example:

My only novel, *The Family Kurasch*, is out of print.

1. Anyone who is fourteen years old faces strong peer pressure every day.

2. Embalming is a technique that preserves a cadaver.

3. The word *chortle* which was invented by Lewis Carroll is a combination of the words *chuckle* and *snort*.

4. The girl standing in the hall outside the classroom is protesting the new rule on school prayer.

5. You should get a carbon monoxide detector if you have a fireplace.

6. My favorite pastime reading Web logs often prevents me from getting enough sleep or doing all my homework.

7. Birds' hearts have four chambers whereas reptiles' have three.

8. Karl Marx an important nineteenth-century political philosopher believed that his role as a social thinker was to change the world.

9. The president elected for a six-year term acts as head of state.

10. The Zuñis an ancient tribe live in New Mexico.

11. Thurgood Marshall the first African American to serve on the U.S. Supreme Court died in 1993.

12. Houses made of wood can often survive earthquakes.

13. Trey Parker and Matt Stone who created *South Park* met as college students in Colorado.

14. The man who rescued her puppy won her eternal gratitude.

15. The tornado which had spared Waterville leveled Douglastown.

42.4 Using commas to set off items in a series

In the following sentences, add any commas that are needed to set off words, phrases, or clauses in a series. If no comma is needed, write C. (See *The Everyday Writer*, pp. 323–324.) Example:

The waiter brought water, menus, and an attitude.
                                    ^   ^

1. From his new job, Jake wanted money prestige and a challenge, in that order.

2. I am looking forward to turning eighteen being able to vote and perhaps serving in the military.

3. The spider's orange body resembles a colored dot amidst eight long black legs.

4. The moon circles the earth the earth revolves around the sun and the sun is just one star among many in the Milky Way galaxy.

5. The ball sailed over the fence across the road and through the Wilsons' window.

6. Ellen is an accomplished freelance writer.

7. They found employment in truck driving farming and mining.

8. The firm's quiet pleasant excessively polite public relations executives made everyone a little nervous.

9. James Joyce wrote novels short stories and poems.

10. Superficial observation does not provide accurate insight into people's lives—how they feel what they believe in how they respond to others.

42.5 **Using commas to set off parenthetical and transitional expressions, contrasting elements, interjections, direct address, and tag questions**

Revise each of the following sentences, using commas to set off parenthetical and transitional expressions, contrasting elements, interjections, words used in direct address, and tag questions. (See *The Everyday Writer*, pp. 324–325.) Example:

Ladies and gentlemen, thank you for your attention.
                          ^

1. Hey stop ogling that construction worker!

2. Madame President I move to adjourn the meeting.

3. Now we can stitch the seam right?

4. The West in fact has become solidly Republican in presidential elections.

5. Last year I am sorry to say six elms had to be destroyed.

6. Captain Kirk I'm a doctor not a madman.

7. The celebration will alas conclude all too soon.

8. One must consider the society as a whole not just its parts.

9. Her friends did not know about her illness did they?

10. Mary announced, "Kids I want you to clean your rooms not make a bigger mess."

42.6 Using commas with dates, addresses, titles, numbers, and quotations

Revise each of the following sentences, using commas appropriately with dates, addresses and place-names, titles, numbers, and quotations. If no comma is needed in a sentence, write C. (See *The Everyday Writer*, pp. 325–327.) Example:

The wine store's original location was 2373 Broadway, New York City.
                                                     ^

1. James Baldwin wrote in 1953 "This world is white no longer, and it will never be white again."

2. Who remarked that "youth is wasted on the young"?

3. "The public be damned!" William Henry Vanderbilt was reported to have said. "I'm working for my stockholders."

4. "Who can match the desperate humorlessness of the adolescent who thinks he is the first to discover seriousness?", asks P. J. Kavanaugh.

5. MLA headquarters are at 10 Astor Place New York New York 10003.

6. The ship was hit by two torpedoes on May 7 1915 and sank in minutes.

7. On the tomb, under the name *Rev. Martin Luther King Jr.*, is a quotation from a famous speech: "Free at last, free at last, thank God almighty I'm free at last."

8. "Neat people are lazier and meaner than sloppy people" according to Suzanne Britt.

9. Ithaca New York has a population of about 30000.

10. In my dictionary, the rules of punctuation begin on page 1560.

42.7 Eliminating unnecessary and inappropriate commas

Revise each of the following sentences, deleting unnecessary commas. If a sentence contains no unnecessary commas, write C. (See *The Everyday Writer*, pp. 327–328.) Example:

Insomniacs are people̸ who have a hard time sleeping soundly.

1. Contrary to popular belief, insomnia is not simply a matter, of being unable to sleep well at night.

2. Insomniacs do indeed wake up at night, but, studies have demonstrated that they also have trouble napping during the day.

3. Why can't insomniacs sleep soundly at night, or nap when they are tired?

4. In many cases, insomniacs suffer, from anxiety.

5. Doctors and sleep researchers, have long considered anxiety to be a common result of getting too little sleep.

6. However, recent studies indicate that anxiety contributes to sleeplessness, not the other way around.

7. Therapies to help insomniacs, include behavior modification and sleeping pills.

8. Sleep therapists recommend, going to bed at the same time every night, not watching television in bed, and not reading in bed.

9. Restless, disturbed, sleep habits are certainly irritating, but are they also, bad for an insomniac's health?

10. While tired people are more dangerous drivers, and less productive workers, no one knows for certain, if insomnia can actually make them sick.

43.1 Using semicolons to link clauses

Combine each of the following pairs of sentences into one sentence by using a semicolon. (See *The Everyday Writer,* pp. 329–331.) Example:

; meet
Take the bus to Henderson Street; ~~Meet~~ me under the clock.

1. City life offers many advantages. In many ways, however, life in a small town is much more pleasant.

2. Teenagers today don't spend all their time on the telephone. Instead, they go online and send each other instant messages.

3. Voltaire was concerned about the political implications of his skepticism. He warned his friends not to discuss atheism in front of the servants.

4. The unwanted package arrived C.O.D. I politely refused to pay the charges.

5. Current celebrities don't have to make fools of themselves on reality television shows. Former celebrities jump at the chance.

6. Pittsburgh was once notorious for its smoke and grime. Today, its skies and streets are cleaner than those of many other American cities.

7. I used to see nothing but woods when I looked out my back window. The view was nothing like it is now, a treeless expanse of new houses.

8. Establishing your position in an office is an important task. Your profile will mold your relationships with other staff members.

9. *Propaganda* is defined as the spread of ideas to further a cause. Therefore, *propaganda* and *advertisement* are synonyms.

10. Florida's mild winter climate is ideal for bicycling. In addition, the terrain is very flat.

43.2 Eliminating misused semicolons

Revise each of the following sentences to correct the misuse of semi-colons. (See *The Everyday Writer*, p. 331.) Example:

The new system would encourage high school students to take more

academic courses;/‚thus strengthening college preparation.

1. We must find a plan to provide decent health care; a necessity in today's life.

2. Verbal scores have decreased by more than fifty-four points; while math scores have decreased by more than thirty-six.

3. For four glorious but underpaid weeks; I'll be working in Yosemite this summer.

4. Finally, I found her at the Humane Society; a beautiful shepherd-collie mix who likes children and plays well with cats.

5. If the North had followed up its victory at Gettysburg more vigorously; the Civil War might have ended sooner.

6. He left a large estate; which was used to endow a scholarship fund.

7. Some gardeners want; low-maintenance plants, limited grass to mow, and low water usage.

8. You can't take your ball and go home; just because you think you'll lose the game.

9. After school; many fourteen-year-olds head to the mall; where they spend the rest of the day.

10. The speech made sense to some observers; but not to me.

44.1 Using periods appropriately

Revise each of the following items, inserting periods in the appropriate places and eliminating any inappropriate punctuation. (See *The Everyday Writer*, pp. 332–333.) Example:

> **Dr. Sarah Blaffer Hrdy has been studying the maternal instinct in**
>   ^
> **humans and other animals.**
>   ^

1. Dr Hrdy, an anthropologist, has studied primate motherhood for many years.

2. She has raised disturbing questions about why parents sometimes kill their offspring?

3. Parents since the Neolithic period of 10,000 BCE have delayed naming infants or otherwise committing to raising them until a few days after birth.

4. Human parents, even in recent centuries, may actively or passively have limited their children's chances to grow up!

5. Dr Hrdy believes that parents may commit infanticide in order to give their other children a better chance

6. The term "parent-offspring conflict" was coined by Robert Trivers, PhD?

7. The popular view of motherhood is that mothers always love their children unconditionally

8. Many mothers are indeed willing to put up with a great deal from their children, from 2.00 A.M. feedings through requests for college tuition.

9. Dr Hrdy asks whether the "maternal instinct" is really instinctive?

10. Describing a mother's crime against her child as "inhuman" is neither accurate nor helpful in preventing future tragedies!

44.2 Using question marks appropriately

Revise each of the following sentences, adding question marks, substituting question marks for other punctuation where appropriate, and removing inappropriately placed question marks. Some sentences do not require any question marks; for those sentences, write C. (See *The Everyday Writer*, p. 333.) Example:

> She asked the travel agent, "What is the air fare to Greece?/"

1. The reporter asked whether the president could explain his proposal in simpler terms?

2. "Can I play this" asked Manuel.

3. Did you just say, "What time is it?"?

4. "How long are we supposed to wait for Sara," wondered Erin?

5. Who said, "Give me liberty, or give me death?"

6. She asked the officer if she could call her lawyer.

7. "Have you heard the one about the tourist and the barber," he asked.

8. What do you think of your new office? your new salary?

9. We began to ask what might fix the problem—restarting the computer, closing other programs, using a different browser.

10. The judge asked, "What is your verdict."

44.3 Using exclamation points appropriately

Revise each of the following sentences, adding or deleting exclamation points as necessary and removing any other inappropriate punctuation that you find. (See *The Everyday Writer*, p. 334.) Example:

> Look out/ the tide is coming in fast/ !
>   ! The

1. The defendant stood up in the witness box and shouted, "I didn't do it. You've got to believe me."

2. Oh, no. We've lost the house.

3. The child cried, "Ouch" as her mother pulled off the bandage!

4. "Go! Go! Go!," roared the crowd as the quarterback sped toward the end zone.

5. What, exactly, do you want!?

6. It was an ordinary school day, so the child once again came home to an empty house!

7. Stop, thief.

8. She exclaimed, "It's too hot."

9. The only thing the surprised guest of honor could say was, "Well, I'll be!".

10. "This is ridiculous," sputtered the diner as the waiter brought the wrong order again!

45.1 Using apostrophes to signal possession

Complete each of the following sentences by inserting 's or an apostrophe alone to form the possessive case of the italicized words. (See *The Everyday Writer*, pp. 335–336.) Example:

Many Internet scare stories are nothing but old *wives*ˌtales.

1. Internet rumors circulate widely because of *people* good intentions.

2. Recipients who pass on messages want everyone to hear about a *child* inspiring fight against cancer or about some dangerous drug, product, or disease.

3. The *Internet* power to inform is great, but so is its power to play tricks on unsuspecting people.

4. A *hoax* creators count on *recipients* kind hearts and concern for the well-being of their families and friends.

5. *Consumers* fears fuel some of the Internet medical scares.

6. Have you heard the one about how *deodorants* ingredients supposedly clog your pores and cause cancer?

7. Another scare warned that sugar substitutes caused the *body* immune system to malfunction.

8. Some of these scares are probably intended to damage certain *corporations* reputations by spreading rumors about products.

9. Others, like the one about checking your toilet seat to be sure it has not become a deadly *spider* hiding place, probably begin as jokes.

10. The *Internet* speed has made such anonymous rumors spread more rapidly than anyone would have thought possible twenty years ago.

45.2   Using apostrophes to create contractions

Revise each of the following sentences so that it uses contractions. Remove any misused apostrophes. (See *The Everyday Writer,* p. 336.) Example:

> That's
> ~~That is~~ the classical music used in the movie *Elvira Madigan.*

1. She does not dislike him, but she would not say that he is her favorite person, either.

2. I cannot believe you have not started the paper yet; it is due tomorrow morning.

3. Who will the critics identify as the best new novelist of the decade?

4. That guy who has been giving you a ride after work called at about nine o'clock.

5. For the test you will be taking on Monday, you are required to have a pencil with No. 2 lead.

6. The clothes that I am washing now did not really get too dirty.

7. The caller says he has been waiting an hour for his pizzas, but we do not have any record of his order.

8. The distributor says that your order has not received it's approval from the business office.

9. It is true that a snake can shed it's own skin and can swallow much of it's prey whole.

10. Is not that the new jazz club that is open on weekends?

46.1   Using quotation marks to signal direct quotation

In the following sentences, add quotation marks each time someone else's exact words are being used. Some sentences do not require quotation marks; mark correct sentences C. (See *The Everyday Writer,* pp. 337–338.) Example:

    "
    Your phone's ringing! **"** **yelled Phil from the end of the hall.**
    ^   ^

1. Although many people believe that Rick says Play it again, Sam, in *Casablanca,* those exact words do not appear in the film.

2. After a tornado ripped through her house, a tearful Indiana woman said she had nothing left.

3. The county employment office's annual summary states that the current unemployment rate is 37 percent lower than it was five years ago.

4. To repeat their words, the worst is behind us.

5. Call me Ishmael is the first sentence of novelist Herman Melville's *Moby Dick*.

6. Most people like to think of themselves as open-minded and flexible enough to change when the circumstances demand.

7. After repeating I can't hear you with her fingers stuck in her ears, Hannah ran to her room and slammed the door.

8. I could not believe the condition of my hometown, he wrote.

9. Keep your opinions to yourselves, Dad muttered as he served the lumpy oatmeal.

10. Is the computer plugged in? the technical support operator asked, prompting Harry to snarl, Yes, I'm not a complete idiot.

46.2 Using quotation marks for definitions and titles

Revise each of the following sentences, using quotation marks appropriately to signal titles and definitions. (See *The Everyday Writer*, pp. 339–340.) Example:

> **The Chinese American businessman surprised his guest by using the Hebrew word *shalom*, which means "peace."**

1. The slogan for the Center for a New American Dream is appropriately simple: More Fun, Less Stuff.

2. My dictionary defines *isolation* as the quality or state of being alone.

3. Two *ER* episodes, Chaos Theory and Freefall, featured Dr. Romano having a run-in with a helicopter.

4. Kowinski uses the term *mallaise* to mean physical and psychological disturbances caused by mall contact.

5. In Flannery O'Connor's short story *Revelation*, colors symbolize passion, violence, sadness, and even God.

6. "The little that is known about gorillas certainly makes you want to know more," writes Alan Moorehead in his essay A Most Forgiving Ape.

7. The British, the guide told us, knit sweaters for their teapots.

8. If you had ever had Stairway to Heaven running through your head for four days straight, you would not like Led Zeppelin either.

9. Big Bill, a section of Dos Passos's book *U.S.A.*, opens with a birth.

10. Amy Lowell challenges social conformity in her poem Patterns.

46.3 Using quotation marks appropriately

Revise each of the following sentences, deleting quotation marks used inappropriately, moving those placed incorrectly, and changing wording as necessary. (See *The Everyday Writer*, pp. 337–342.) Example:

Do advertisements /really/ have something to teach us about our culture?

1. Cable channels like "Nickelodeon" include what they term "classic" commercials as part of the programming.

2. Television commercials have frequently used "popular" songs as an effective way to connect their product with good feelings in consumers' minds.

3. Many middle-aged Americans still associate the wee-oo sound of the theremin from the Beach Boys' Good Vibrations with images of beach-goers enjoying orange soft drinks.

4. The strategy of using hit songs in commercials can "backfire" when the listeners don't like the song or like it too much to think of it as an advertising "jingle."

5. Many aging baby boomers were disturbed to hear "Beatles" songs being used to sell shoes.

6. The rights to many Beatles songs, such as "Revolution", are no longer controlled by the Beatles.

7. Sometimes advertisements contain songs that seem to have no connection at all to the products being "plugged."

8. Many Iggy Pop fans wonder what on earth his song Lust for Life has to do with taking an expensive ocean cruise.

9. Not surprisingly, the song's more peculiar lyrics, including Well, that's like hypnotizing chickens, are omitted from the cruise-line advertisements.

10. Do consumers love the songs of their youth so much that merely "hearing" a song in an ad will make them buy that car?

47.1 Using parentheses and brackets

Revise the following sentences, using parentheses and brackets correctly. Change any other punctuation in the sentences as needed. (See *The Everyday Writer,* pp. 344–345.) Example:

> Since the disputed presidential election of 2000, many observers
>
> (and not just from right-wing media outlets)have argued that U.S.
>   ^   ^
> journalists are not doing a thorough job of presenting political issues.

1. The words *media elite* have been said so often usually by people who are themselves elite members of the media that the phrase has taken on a life of its own.

2. Are the media really elite, and are they really liberal, as talk-show regulars (Ann Coulter, for example argue)?

3. Media critic Eric Alterman has coined the term "so-called liberal media" [SCLM] because he believes that the media have been intimidated by criticism.

4. An article in the *Journal of Communication* discussing the outcome of recent U.S. elections explained that "claiming the media are liberally biased perhaps has become a core rhetorical strategy" used by conservatives, qtd. in Alterman 14.

5. Some progressive groups (including Fairness and Accuracy in Reporting (FAIR)) keep track of media coverage of political issues and campaigns.

6. However, liberals are not the only media watchdogs: right-wing organizations, including Accuracy in Media, (AIM) also closely examine the way political stories are reported.

7. The nonpartisan Campaign Desk Web site [sponsored by the *Columbia Journalism Review*] was dedicated to tracking media coverage of the 2004 presidential election.

8. According to the site's home page, the purpose of Campaign Desk was "to straighten and deepen campaign coverage" as a resource for voters (most of whom rely on media coverage to make decisions about the candidates.)

9. Is truly objective coverage of hot-button issues and political candidates, (whether Republicans or Democrats,) ever possible?

10. And can we forget that as media consumers, we have an obligation to be an informed electorate (even though it's easy to pay attention only to the news that reinforces our own beliefs.)?

47.2 Using dashes

Revise the following sentences so that dashes are used correctly. If the sentence is correct as written, write C. (See *The Everyday Writer*, pp. 345–346.) Example:

In some states‾California, for example‾banks are no longer allowed to
          ^   ^
charge ATM users an additional fee for withdrawing money.

1. Many consumers accept the fact that they have to pay additional fees for services like bank machines if they don't want to pay, they don't have to use the service.

2. Nevertheless, — extra charges seem to be added to more and more services all the time.

3. Some of the charges are ridiculous why should hotels charge guests a fee for making a toll-free telephone call?

4. The hidden costs of service fees are irritating people feel that their bank accounts are being nibbled to death.

5. But some of the fees consumers are asked to pay — are more than simply irritating.

6. The "convenience charges" — that people have to pay when buying show tickets by telephone — are often a substantial percentage of the cost of the ticket.

7. If ticket buyers don't want to pay these "convenience charges" and who does? they must buy their tickets at the box office.

8. Finally, there are government fees that telephone companies and other large corporations are required to pay.

9. Telephone companies routinely pass these fees used to ensure Internet access to remote areas and schools along to their customers, implying that the government expects consumers to pay.

10. Many consumers are not aware that the government requires the corporations — not the general public — to pay these fees.

47.3 Using colons

Insert a colon in each of the following items that needs one. Some of the items do not require a colon; if the sentence is correct as written, write *C*. (See *The Everyday Writer*, pp. 346–347.) Example:

> Some fans of the *Star Wars* films have created a new online version of
>
> *Episode I* : *The Phantom Menace* that deletes all of the scenes with Jar
>   ^
> Jar Binks.

1. Gandhi urged four rules tell the truth even in business, adopt more sanitary habits, abolish caste and religious divisions, and learn English.

2. Solid vocal technique is founded on the correct use of head position, diaphragm control, muscle relaxation, and voice placement.

3. Another example is taken from Psalm 139 16.

4. The sonnet's structure is effective in revealing the speaker's message love has changed his life and ended his depression.

5. The article "Slim Pickings Looking beyond Ephedra" explains that few legal drugs promote weight loss.

6. Even more important was what money represented success, prestige, and power.

7. Voters rejected the school budget increase by a 2,1 margin, leaving school officials wondering how to cope with classroom overcrowding.

8. Education can alleviate problems such as poverty, poor health, and the energy shortage.

9. Doug and I both asked ourselves the same question "What happens if one of us gets sick?"

10. Reviewers agree that Lisa's book possesses these traits readability, intelligence, and usefulness.

47.4 Using ellipses

Read the following passage. Then assume that the underlined portions have been left out in a reprinting of the passage. Indicate how you would use ellipses to indicate those deletions. (See *The Everyday Writer*, pp. 348–349.) Example:

> . . .
> **Saving money is difficult ~~for young people in entry-level positions,~~**
>   ^
> **but it is important.**

Should young people <u>who are just getting started in their careers</u> think about saving for retirement? Those who begin to save in their twenties <u>are making a wise financial decision. They</u> are putting away money that can earn compound interest for decades. Even if they save only a hundred dollars a month, and even if they stop saving when they hit age thirty-five, the total forty years later will be impressive. <u>On the other hand,</u> people who wait until they are fifty to begin saving will have far less money put aside at the age of sixty-five. People who wait too long may face an impoverished retirement <u>unless they are able to save thousands of dollars each month.</u> Of course, no one knows how long he or she will live, but saving is a way of gambling on reaching retirement. Difficult as it may be to think about being sixty-five or seventy years old, young people should plan ahead.

47.5 Reviewing punctuation marks

Correct the punctuation in the following sentences. If the punctuation is already correct, write C. (See *The Everyday Writer*, pp. 318–349.) Example:

> **Children⁄ who are too young to speak⁄ are often frustrated because they cannot communicate their wishes.**

1. Many American parents are willing to try almost anything prenatal music, infant flash cards, you name it to help their children succeed.

2. Some parental efforts do help children, for instance, children whose parents read to them are more likely to enjoy books.

3. Other schemes to make babies smarter, such as the so-called *Mozart effect*, apparently don't make much difference.

4. A new idea that is "popular" with many parents of young children is sign language.

5. Researcher Joseph Garcia an expert in child development and in American Sign Language noticed that hearing babies with deaf parents often learned sign language before they could speak.

6. By sixteen to eighteen months, most children are able to speak simple words, and make themselves understood.

7. However, babies can communicate simple ideas to their parents starting at about eight months, if the infants learn signs.

8. Garcia showed that parents could easily teach their children signs for words like please, more, sleepy, and hungry.

9. Garcia wrote a book called "Sign with Your Baby."

10. Not surprisingly, parents bought the book, (and then the video,) and now sign-language classes for small children are easy to find.

11. Parents who go to signing classes with their infants and toddlers hope for a good outcome; better communication between parent and child and less frustration for both.

12. A study by California researchers found that seven-year-olds earned slightly higher IQ scores if they had learned to sign as infants.

13. It's not surprising that this studys results fueled the demand for more toddler sign-language classes.

14. The researchers who developed the study said that the best reason for parents to sign with their children was to allow the children "to communicate what they need and see".

15. One researcher, Dr Elizabeth Bates, told the "New York Times" that the hand movements that small children can learn are really gestures, not proper sign language.

16. Others contend that the childrens' hand movements stand for concepts so the movements are sign language.

17. Some parents fear that a child who learns to communicate by signs will have little incentive to speak researchers have found no evidence of this effect.

18. In fact children who can use sign language are often especially eager to learn how to speak.

19. While signing appears to have some benefits for the children who learn it not everyone feels that parents need to rush out to attend a class.

20. Any activity that gets parents to spend more time communicating with their children probably has it's benefits.

48.1 Capitalizing

Capitalize words as needed in the following sentences. (See *The Everyday Writer*, pp. 350–354.) Example:

T S E   T   W   L   F,
ȶ. ȿ. ȿliot, who wrote ȶhe ᴡaste ȴand, was an editor at ȴaber
          F
and ȴaber.

1. johnny depp appeared to be having a wonderful time playing captain jack sparrow in *pirates of the caribbean: the curse of the black pearl.*

2. the battle of lexington and concord was fought in april 1775.

3. i will cite the novels of vladimir nabokov, in particular *pnin* and *lolita*.

4. accepting an award for his score for the film *the high and the mighty*, dmitri tiomkin thanked beethoven, brahms, wagner, and strauss.

5. i wondered if my new levi's were faded enough.

6. We drove east over the hudson river on the tappan zee bridge.

7. senator trent lott was widely criticized after appearing to praise senator strom thurmond's segregationist past.

8. "bloody sunday" was a massacre of catholic protesters in derry, northern ireland, on january 30, 1972.

9. we had a choice of fast-food, chinese, or italian restaurants.

10. the town in the American south where i was raised had a statue of a civil war soldier in the center of main street.

49.1 Using abbreviations

Revise each of the following sentences to eliminate any abbreviations that would be inappropriate in academic writing. (See *The Everyday Writer*, pp. 355–357.) Example:

international
The ~~intl.~~ sport of belt sander racing began in a hardware store.

1. Nielson Hardware in Point Roberts, WA, was the site of the world's first belt sander race in 1989.

2. The power tools, ordinarily used for sanding wood, are placed on a thirty-ft. track and plugged in; the sander to reach the end first wins.

3. Today, the International Belt Sander Drag Race Association (IBSDRA) sponsors tours of winning sanders, an international championship, and a Web site that sells IBSDRA T-shirts.

4. There are three divisions of belt sander races: the stock div., which races sanders right out of the box; the modified div., which allows any motor the owner wants to add; and the decorative div., which provides a creative outlet for sander owners.

5. An average race lasts two seconds, but the world champion modified sander raced the track in 1.52 secs.

6. The fastest sanders run on very coarse sandpaper—a no. sixteen grit is an excellent choice if it's available.

7. Stock sanders are usually widely available brands, e.g., Mikita or Bosch.

8. The S-B Power Tool Co. in Chicago, maker of Bosch sanders, allows participants to race its tools, but the co. does not underwrite races.

9. Another tool company, the Do It Best Corp. of Wayne, Ind., sponsors races across the U.S. and Canada.

10. No one knows what % of the nation's power tools have been used for this kind of entertainment.

49.2 Spelling out numbers and using figures

Revise the numbers in the following sentences as necessary for correctness and consistency. If a sentence is correct, write C. (See *The Everyday Writer*, pp. 358–359.) Example:

seventh   one

No correct answer choice was given for the ~~7th~~ question in part ~~1~~ of the test.

1. In the 35-to-44 age group, the risk is estimated to be about 1 in 2,500.

2. You could travel around the city for only 65 cents.

3. The amulet measured one and one-eighth by two and two-fifths inches.

4. Walker signed a three-year, $4.5-million contract.

5. The morning of September eleven, 2001, was cool and clear in New York City.

6. The parents considered twenty-five cents enough of an allowance for a five-year-old.

7. I drank 8 glasses of water, as the doctor had said, but then I had to get up 3 times during the night.

8. 307 miles long and 82 miles wide, the island offered little of interest.

9. Cable TV is now available to seventy-two percent of the population.

10. The department received 1,633 calls and forty-three letters.

50.1 Using italics

In each of the following sentences, underline any words that should be italicized, and circle any italicized words that should not be. If a title requires quotation marks instead of italicization, add them. (See *The Everyday Writer,* pp. 359–361.) Example:

> **The United States still abounds with regional speech — for example, many people in the Appalachians still use local words such as <u>crick</u> and <u>holler</u>.**

1. *Regionalism,* a nineteenth-century literary movement, focused on the language and customs of people in areas of the country not yet affected by industrialization.

2. Regional writers produced some American classics, such as Mark Twain's Huckleberry Finn and James Fenimore Cooper's Last of the Mohicans.

3. Twain, not an admirer of Cooper's work, wrote a scathing essay about his predecessor called *The Literary Offenses of James Fenimore Cooper.*

4. Some of the most prolific regional writers were women like Kate Chopin, who wrote her first collection of short stories, Bayou Folk, to help support her family.

5. The stories in *Bayou Folk,* such as the famous *Désirée's Baby,* focus on the natives of rural Louisiana.

6. Chopin also departed from regional works to explore women's experiences of marriage, as in her short piece, *The Story of an Hour.*

7. In Maine, Sarah Orne Jewett wrote sketches of rural life that appeared in the Atlantic Monthly.

8. She later turned these into a novel, Deephaven, which she hoped would "teach the world that country people were not . . . ignorant."

9. Her finest short story, *A White Heron,* and her celebrated novel *The Country of the Pointed Firs* also benefit from settings in Maine.

10. Many regional stories—Stephen Crane's *The Bride Comes to Yellow Sky* is a prime example—show the writer's concern that an isolated culture is in danger of disappearing.

51.1 Using hyphens in compounds and with prefixes

Insert hyphens as needed. A dictionary will help you with some items. If an item does not require a hyphen, write C. (See *The Everyday Writer,* pp. 362–364.) Example:

full̄ bodied wine
   ⌃

1. pro and anti-World Trade Organization marchers

2. thirty three

3. pre World War II

4. a politician who is fast talking

5. a hard working farmer

6. a what me worry look

7. deescalate

8. self guided

9. happily married couple

10. professor emeritus

51.2 Using hyphens appropriately

Insert or delete hyphens as necessary, and revise any incorrect word divisions in the following sentences. Use your dictionary if necessary. If a sentence is correct as printed, write C. (See *The Everyday Writer,* pp. 362–364.) Example:

The bleary ̄eyed student finally (stop⁄)
           ⌃
/**ped fighting sleep and went to bed.**
⌃

1. The carpenter asked for a two pound bag of three quarter inch nails.

2. The name of the president elect had been announced an hour before the polls closed.

3. We urged him to be open minded and to temper his insensitive views.

4. Stress can lead to hypertension and ulcers.

5. Her dolllike features fooled many observers, but her competitors soon found that she had ice-cold blood and nerves-of-steel.

6. In Bizet's *Carmen,* the ill-fated Carmen is betrayed by her fic-kleness.

7. The drum-beating and hand-clapping signaled that the parade was near.

8. The badly-wrapped sandwich oozed mustard and bits of soggy lettuce.

9. Suicide among teenagers has tripled in the past thirty five years.

10. One of Baryshnikov's favorite dancers was none other than Fred A-staire.

For Multilingual Writers

64.1 Identifying count and noncount nouns

Identify each of the common nouns in the following short paragraph as either a count or a noncount noun. (See *The Everyday Writer*, pp. 495–496.) The first one has been done for you.

In his book *Hiroshima*, John Hersey tells the story of six people who survived the destruction of Hiroshima on August 6, 1945. The bomb detonated at 8:15 in the morning. When the explosion occurred, Mrs. Hatsuyo Nakamura was looking out her window and watching a neighbor at work on his house. The force of the explosion lifted her into the air and carried her into the next room, where she was buried by roofing tiles and other debris. When she crawled out, she heard her daughter, Myeko, calling out; she was buried up to her waist and could not move.

64.2 Using appropriate determiners; stating plural forms explicitly

Each of the following sentences contains an error with a noun phrase. Revise each sentence. (See *The Everyday Writer*, pp. 496–497.) Example:

Many people use small sponge to clean their kitchen counters.

1. Bacteria are invisible organisms that can sometimes make the people sick.

2. Dangerous germs such as salmonella are commonly found in a some foods.

3. When a cook prepares chicken on cutting board, salmonella germs may be left on the board.

4. Much people regularly clean their kitchen counters and cutting boards to remove bacteria.

5. Unfortunately, a warm, wet kitchen sponge is a ideal home for bacteria.

6. Every time someone wipes a counter with dirty sponge, more germ are spread around the kitchen.

7. Microwaving a dirty sponge for one minute will kill a most bacteria that live in it.

8. According to research studies, the young single men's kitchens tend to have a fewer germs than many other kitchen.

9. These surprising fact tells researchers that young single men do not often wipe their kitchen counters.

10. To eliminate dangerous many bacteria from the kitchen, a cooks should wash their hands frequently.

64.3   Using articles appropriately

Insert articles as necessary in the following passage. If no article is needed, leave the space blank. (See *The Everyday Writer*, pp. 497–499.) Example:

One of ____the____ things that makes _____ English unique is

____the____ number of _____ English words.

_____ English language has _____ very large vocabulary.

About _____ 200,000 words are in _____ everyday use, and if

_____ less common words are included, _____ total reaches

more than _____ million. This makes _____ English

_____ rich language, but also _____ difficult one to learn well.

In addition, _____ rules of English grammar are sometimes confus-

ing. They were modeled on _____ Latin rules, even though

_____ two languages are very different. Finally, _____ fact that

_____ English has _____ large number of _____ words

imported from _____ other languages makes _____ English

spelling very hard to master. _____ English is now _____ most

widely used language around _____ world, so _____ educated

people are expected to know it.

64.4 Positioning modifiers

Possible modifiers for each of the following nouns are listed alpha-
betically in parentheses after the noun. Indicate the order in which
the adjectives should precede the noun. (See *The Everyday Writer*, pp.
499–500.) Example:

> <u>Popular New Orleans jazz</u> **album (jazz/New Orleans/popular)**

1. _____ novel (new/Spanish/well-received)

2. _____ park (amusement/deserted/large)

3. _____ couch (futon/sagging)

4. _____ encyclopedia (multivolume/valuable)

5. _____ cloud (threatening/storm)

6. _____ team (coed/volleyball)

7. _____ cloth (batik/orange/unusual)

8. _____ program (educational/worthwhile)

9. _____ pumpkin (orange/fat)

10. _____ rental (movie/X-rated)

65.1 Using the present, the present perfect, and the past forms of verbs

Rewrite the following passage by adding appropriate forms of *have* and main-verb endings or forms for the verbs in parentheses. (See *The Everyday Writer,* pp. 501–505.) Example:

I _____ like _____ (like) to try new foods, so I ____ have eaten ____

(eat) in many different kinds of restaurants in my life.

Several times, I _____ (hear) people musing about the

bravery of the first person who ever _____ (eat) a lobster. It

_____ (be) an interesting question: What do you

_____ (think) _____ (make) anyone do such a

thing? But personally, I _____ (wonder) all my life about how

ancient people _____ (discover) the art of baking bread. After

all, preparing a lobster _____ (be) pretty simple in comparison

to baking. Bread _____ (feed) vast numbers of people for

centuries, so it certainly _____ (be) a more important food

source than lobster, too. Those of us who _____ (love) either

lobster or bread (or both) _____ (be) grateful to those who

_____ (give) us such a wonderful culinary legacy.

65.2 Using specified forms of verbs

Using the subjects and verbs provided, write the specified sentences. (See *The Everyday Writer,* pp. 501–505.) Example:

subject: *Bernie* **verb:** *touch*
sentence using a present form: Bernie touches the soft fur.
sentence using the auxiliary verb *had*: Bernie had touched a squid before.

1. subject: *they* verb: *decide*

   sentence using a present form:

   sentence using an auxiliary verb + the past participle form:

2. subject: *someone* verb: *follow*

   sentence using a past form:

   sentence using an auxiliary verb + the present participle form:

3. subject: *we* verb: *ask*

   sentence using a present form:

   sentence using the auxiliary *had* + the past participle form:

4. subject: *geese* verb: *migrate*

   sentence using a past form:

   sentence using an auxiliary verb + the present participle form:

5. subject: *baby* verb: *sleep*

   sentence using a present form:

   sentence using an auxiliary verb + past participle form:

6. subject: *teenagers* verb: *consume*

   sentence using a past form:

   sentence using the auxiliary verb *were* + the present participle form:

7. subject: *judge* verb: *expect*

   sentence using a present form:

   sentence using an auxiliary verb + a present participle form:

8. subject: *pasta* verb: *steam*

   sentence using a past form:

   sentence using an auxiliary verb + present participle form:

9. subject: *pilots* verb: *fly*

   sentence using a past form:

   sentence using an auxiliary verb + a present participle form:

10. subject: *hamburger* verb: *taste*

    sentence using a present form:

    sentence using an auxiliary verb + a past participle form:

65.3 Identifying tenses and forms of verbs

From the following list, identify the form of each verb or verb phrase in each of the numbered sentences. (See *The Everyday Writer*, pp. 501–505.)

simple present	past perfect
simple past	present progressive
present perfect	past progressive

Example:

> **Judge Cohen considered the two arguments.** Simple past

1. On the right side of the room, Monica is demonstrating the Heimlich maneuver.

2. Your children were talking throughout the entire movie.

3. She is exercising to reduce stress.

4. As guests were arriving, Cheryl was still getting dressed.

5. Just as we took our seats, the movie began.

6. I have attempted that math problem several times now.

7. Paul required special medical attention for years.

8. My mother has driven the same Mazda for ten years.

9. Horror movies rarely make much of an impression on me, but this one has made me afraid to go out into the parking lot.

10. She had forgotten the assignment.

65.4 Using verbs appropriately

Each of the following sentences contains an error with verbs. Revise each sentence. (See *The Everyday Writer*, pp. 500–507.) Example:

>   could not
> **Linguists ~~cannot~~ interpret hieroglyphics before they discovered the**
>   ^
> **Rosetta Stone.**

1. A French engineer was finding a stone half-buried in the mud by the Nile River in Egypt in 1799.

2. The Rosetta Stone is cover with inscriptions in three ancient languages.

3. The inscription at the top of the stone written in Egyptian hieroglyphics, or pictographs, while the lower part gives the same information in an ancient Egyptian language called Demotic and in ancient Greek.

4. At that time, scholars were puzzled by hieroglyphics for centuries.

5. Very soon after its discovery, the French have made copies of the stone.

6. A scholar named Jean François Champollion could understood both ancient Greek and modern Egyptian, known as Coptic.

7. Champollion knew that he can figure out the Demotic script based on his knowledge of Coptic.

8. From the Coptic inscription, he has learned to read the hieroglyphics.

9. The story of the Rosetta Stone is probably more fascinated than the contents of its inscription.

10. The hieroglyphics, Demotic, and Greek texts all are containing a decree from an ancient king.

66.1 Using prepositions idiomatically

Insert one or more appropriate prepositions in each of the following sentences. (See *The Everyday Writer*, p. 508.) Example:

We will have the answer ___ by ___ four o'clock this afternoon.

1. Children should have pencils _____ their pencil cases.

2. How can schools help when children arrive _____ the morning without breakfast?

3. Education requires participation _____ all of us.

4. Children should fall _____ love with reading.

5. Adults who read to children can provide good examples _____ them.

6. Students should get to school precisely _____ time.

7. Having someone to help them _____ home gives struggling students more confidence.

8. Schools themselves may be struggling _____ financial cutbacks and poor facilities.

9. Classrooms need books _____ their shelves.

10. A high-quality public education should be given _____ every child.

66.2 Recognizing and using two-word verbs

Identify each italicized expression as either a two-word verb or a verb + preposition. (See *The Everyday Writer,* pp. 508–511.) Example:

Look *up* John Brown the next time you're in town.   two-word verb

1. George was still *looking for* his keys when we left.

2. I always *turn down* the thermostat when I go to bed or leave the house.

3. We drank a pitcher of lemonade in an attempt to *cool* ourselves *off* on a sweltering July afternoon.

4. Marion *gave back* the ring she had gotten as an engagement gift.

5. Jimmy *takes after* his father, poor thing.

6. The car *turned into* the driveway.

7. The frog *turned into* a prince.

8. The camp counselor *handed* the candy *out* as if it were gold.

9. *Put* the garbage *out* on the sidewalk, please.

10. Don't *put* yourself *out* on my behalf.

67.1 Expressing subjects and objects explicitly

Revise the following sentences or nonsentences so that they have explicit subjects and objects as necessary. If a sentence does not contain an error, write C. (See *The Everyday Writer*, pp. 511–512.) Example:

It is
I̶s̶ easy and convenient for people with access to computers to shop
^
online.

1. No faster way to take care of holiday shopping.

2. Computers also allow people to buy items they cannot find locally.

3. Banks and credit-card companies have Web sites now, and consumers use for making payments, looking at statements, and transferring balances.

4. Are problems with doing everything online, of course.

5. Customers must use credit cards, and thieves want to break in and get.

6. Are small-time thieves and juvenile pranksters disrupting online services.

7. Jamming popular sites is one way for hackers to gain notoriety, and have been several such actions.

8. A hacker can get enormous amounts of online data, even if is supposed to be secure.

9. People have every right to be concerned about online privacy, for is a tremendous amount of private information stored in online databases, including medical records and financial data.

10. Internet users must use caution and common sense online, but is also essential for online information to be safeguarded by security experts.

67.2   Editing for English word order

Revise the following sentences as necessary. If a sentence does not contain an error, write C. (See *The Everyday Writer*, pp. 512–513.) Example:

1. To sleep he wishes to go now.

2. He displays proudly in the window a flag.

3. Comes in first the runner from Kenya.

4. She should go not into the woods alone.

5. A passing grade she wants.

6. Extremely poorly Sandy drove during her first road test.

7. Slow and easy wins the race.

8. Desserts some restaurant guests would like to begin with.

9. John watches videos incessantly.

10. "Speak fluently English," ordered the instructor.

67.3   Using noun clauses, infinitives, and gerunds appropriately

Revise the following sentences as necessary so that each contains an appropriate noun clause, infinitive, or gerund positioned well. If a sentence does not contain an error, write C. (See *The Everyday Writer*, pp. 513–515.) Example:

        that
It pleases me ⌄ you like me.

1. Is important that we think in English.

2. We discussed to go to a movie, but we could not agree on what to see.

3. It annoys the teacher we don't practice conversation.

4. It is possible that you are right.

5. Ashok refused answering his sister's questions.

6. Her mother stopped to drive on her ninetieth birthday.

7. What he has to say is of great interest to me.

8. It is obvious that she made the right decision.

9. No one expected being allowed to leave work before midnight.

10. We appreciated to get the invitation.

67.4 Using adjective clauses carefully

Revise the following sentences so that each includes an appropriate adjective clause that is positioned correctly. Make sure the sentence does not include unnecessary words or omit necessary relative pronouns. If a sentence does not contain an error, write C. (See *The Everyday Writer*, pp. 515–517.) Example:

who
The student works the hardest gains the most.
    ^

1. The class has twenty students in it that I am taking.

2. Some students want to practice speaking more asked us all to help prepare a dinner.

3. The class dinner we cooked together represented food from a dozen countries.

4. A reporter attended the dinner and wrote an article which he praised the chefs in it.

5. The chef works at my club helped by lending us pots and pans.

6. My mother makes many delicious dishes that they come from our homeland.

7. She taught me how to make that I have always loved the fritters called *kofte*.

8. We all come from different places, so those of us were cooking together had to speak English to communicate.

9. The room in that we made our dinner smelled delicious.

10. Spoken English, which I had always found very difficult, is easier for me now.

67.5 Writing conditional sentences

Revise each of the following sentences so that both the *if*-clause and the main, or independent, clause contain appropriate verb forms. If a sentence does not contain an error, write C. (See *The Everyday Writer,* pp. 517–518.) Example:

> If you want to work as a computer programmer, you ~~would~~
>   *are*
> probably ~~be~~ having a hard time finding a high-paying U.S. job
>   ^
> these days.

1. Until recently, many people thought that U.S. computer jobs will go unfilled unless college-educated foreign workers will be allowed to work in this country.

2. If the dot-com boom had continued, that prediction might come true.

3. Instead, many highly skilled U.S. technology workers will have few options if they became unemployed tomorrow.

4. If any computer job is announced these days, hundreds of qualified people applied for it.

5. Today, if a company uses many programmers or other computer experts, it may hire workers in India to fill the positions.

6. If Indian workers would require as much money as Americans do to live, U.S. companies would not be as eager to outsource computer work to the other side of the world.

7. If business owners cared more about keeping good jobs at home, they hired skilled workers here instead of skilled workers in another country.

8. Will fewer Americans be unemployed right now if the dot-com boom had never happened?

9. Some young people in this country would not have gotten useless technology degrees if they knew how the economy would decline.

10. If American students would want to prepare for a secure future, they should consider a specialty like nursing, in which jobs are available and the work cannot be sent abroad.

Answers to the Even-Numbered Exercises

LEARNING FROM COMMON ERRORS

EXERCISE 3.1   Recognizing and eliminating the twenty most common errors

Some sentences have errors that most people would solve the same way; some sentences contain errors that have various solutions. Students may wish to make changes in addition to the corrections noted.

2. Today, we often forget how dangerous childhood diseases can be. Less than a century ago, many children did not survive to adulthood because of diphtheria, whooping cough, and measles. Fortunately, such ailments are rare nowadays; however, if people decide not to immunize their children, these illnesses could easily make a comeback.

4. [The first sentence is missing commas.] I was gaining speed and feeling really good, but when I looked back, he wasn't there.

6. [The error is in the second sentence.] After all, it is they who will support us with things like money, food, and clothes until we are capable of living on our own.

8. [The errors are in the third sentence.] And if you get extremely lost, pulling off and asking will be the easiest way to get on track.

10. [The errors are in the second, third, and fourth sentences.] Setting up entails claiming your own territory, which you do by laying out your oversized beach towel and by turning your radio on loud enough to mark your domain without disturbing anyone else. This action should help you blend in with the locals.

12. [The error is in the second sentence.] He even named his new puppy Einstein, but that didn't prevent the dog from chasing its tail.

14. [The error is in the second sentence.] Those university representatives who argue that students and professors should rely on an honor system believe that investigating student essays does more harm than good.

16. [The error is in the second sentence.] A child in an extremely unhappy home will not necessarily be more miserable if his or her parents divorce.

18. [The error is in the first sentence.] In the attic, we found several old board games that no one remembered how to play.

20. [The error is in the first sentence.] The knights, with armor and horses beautifully decorated, participate in battles of jousting, target shooting with spears, archery, and duels of strategy and strength using swords and shields.

COMPOSING IN A DIGITAL AGE

EXERCISE 10.2 Recognizing logical and emotional fallacies

SUGGESTED ANSWERS

2. *Fallacy:* logical and emotional
   Explanation: The sentence tries to frighten the audience with a threatening vision of the future. It also links financial aid for schools with their ability to turn out students who are not dunces, but it doesn't offer any evidence of such a link.

4. *Fallacy:* logical
   Explanation: This sentence greatly oversimplifies the path to a lucrative career. Simply growing up with a computer is not enough to guarantee a good income.

6. *Fallacy:* logical
   Explanation: The passage states that low self-esteem causes poor grades. However, the fact that the two phenomena often occur at the same time does not prove that one causes the other.

8. *Fallacy:* logical
   Explanation: The sentence treats the question as if it has already been answered, but the fact that the National Rifle Association resists gun control laws does not prove that other Americans will feel the same way.

10. *Fallacy:* emotional
    Explanation: The sentence uses flattery to win readers over to a different brand of toothpaste.

EXERCISE 11.1 Recognizing arguable statements

2. factual

4. factual

6. arguable

8. factual

10. arguable

EXERCISE 11.2   Demonstrating fairness

SUGGESTED ANSWERS

2. The copywriters demonstrate fairness by explaining that the company invests only in socially responsible funds and that it requires an investment minimum of only $250, which makes the company accessible to lower-income investors.

SENTENCE STYLE

EXERCISE 21.1   Matching subjects and predicates

SUGGESTED ANSWERS

2. In her books, many of which deal with the aftermath of slavery, are strong women characters.

   Her books, many of which deal with the aftermath of slavery, often feature strong women characters.

4. Although Morrison's depictions of African American families and neighborhoods are realistic, they also include supernatural elements.

   Morrison's depictions of African American families and neighborhoods are realistic, but they also include supernatural elements.

6. *Song of Solomon* was hailed as a masterpiece, winning the National Book Critics Circle Award in 1978.

   Song of Solomon, hailed as a masterpiece, won the National Book Critics Circle Award in 1978.

8. The title character in *Beloved* is the ghost of a murdered infant inhabiting the body of a young woman.

   Beloved features the ghost of a murdered infant inhabiting the body of a young woman.

10. In 1993, Toni Morrison became the first African American woman to be awarded the Nobel Prize in literature.

    Toni Morrison, who was awarded the Nobel Prize in literature in 1993, was the first African American woman to win that prize.

EXERCISE 21.2   Making comparisons complete, consistent, and clear

SUGGESTED ANSWERS

2. New York City has a more diverse culture than any other metropolis in the United States.

4. As time went on, the baby became less animated and less interested.

6. The car's exterior is blue, but the seats are black vinyl.

8. Are citizens of the United States now as safe as or safer than they were before September 11, 2001?

10. She argued that children are even more important for men than they are for women.

EXERCISE 22.2 Writing sentences with subordination

SUGGESTED ANSWERS

2. At my parents' house, I spent a long night on a sleep sofa that has an uncomfortably thin mattress with a hard metal bar beneath it.

4. Walking into the shelter, I saw men, women, and children slumped against the wall, their belongings lying in overturned shopping carts.

EXERCISE 23.1 Creating parallel words or phrases

SUGGESTED ANSWERS

2. I want not only hot fudge but also whipped cream.

4. I told my younger sister to keep out of my clothes and to keep away from my friends.

6. When he got his promotion, he told the neighbors, called his family, and took out an ad in the newspaper.

8. We must either walk quickly or drive slowly.

10. The contract required the workers to come in late at night and to keep quiet about what they saw.

EXERCISE 23.2 Revising sentences for parallelism

SUGGESTED ANSWERS

2. Many people in this country remember dancing to the mambo music of the 1950s and listening to that era's Latin bands.

4. Growing up near Havana and studying classical piano, Pérez Prado loved Cuban music.

6. Playing piano in Havana nightclubs, arranging music for a Latin big band, and joining jam sessions with the band's guitarists gave him the idea for a new kind of music.

8. Prado conducted his orchestra by waving his hands, moving his head and shoulders, and kicking his feet high in the air.

10. Pérez Prado, an innovator and a great musician, died in 1989.

EXERCISE 24.1   Revising for verb tense and mood

SUGGESTED ANSWERS

2. Correct

4. All health care workers should know that they have to keep their hands clean.

6. Hand-washing can be repetitive, time consuming, and boring, but it is crucial to patient safety in every hospital.

8. The bacteria that cause these infections cannot travel through the air. They require physical contact to move from place to place.

10. Wash your hands frequently, and follow these instructions even if your skin gets dry.

EXERCISE 24.2   Eliminating shifts in voice and point of view

SUGGESTED ANSWERS

2. I liked the sense of individualism, the crowd yelling for *me,* and the feeling that I was in command.

4. When someone says "roommate" to a high school senior bound for college, that senior *conjures up* thoughts of no privacy and potential fights.

6. We knew that we shouldn't walk across the railroad trestle, but we went ahead anyway.

8. *Lionel gathered* the roses, and then he arranged them.

10. Suddenly we heard an explosion of wings off to our right, and *we* could see a hundred or more ducks lifting off from the water.

EXERCISE 24.3   Eliminating shifts between direct and indirect discourse

SUGGESTED ANSWERS

2. She said that during a semester abroad, she really missed all her friends.

4. Loren Eiseley feels an urge to join the birds in their soundless flight, but in the end he knows that he cannot *and that he is only a man.*

EXERCISE 24.4   Eliminating shifts in tone and diction

SUGGESTED ANSWERS

2. The Chinese invented noodles, even though many people think that the Italians created them.

4. The Guggenheim exhibit of African works of art, often misunderstood and undervalued by Western art historians, is a mind-expanding show.

EXERCISE 25.1 Emphasizing main ideas

SUGGESTED ANSWERS

2. Although so-called mad cow disease is extremely rare, people fear it because it eats holes in the brain tissue, depriving its victims of intellect, memory, and life.

4. As the stranded whale wriggled off the sandy beach, a crowd gathered and a chorus of seagulls cried shrilly.

6. Victorian women were warned that smoking would cause them to grow a mustache, contract tuberculosis, become sterile, or die young.

8. Coast Guard personnel conduct boating safety classes, monitor emergency radio channels, and sometimes must risk their own lives to save others.

10. Dr. Carver, who grew up in an impoverished family, achieved his dream of becoming a surgeon. He has separated several pairs of conjoined twins.

EXERCISE 26.1 Eliminating unnecessary words and phrases

SUGGESTED ANSWERS

2. Shortly after Houdini's birth, his family moved to Appleton, where his father served as the only rabbi.

4. His many escapes included getting out of a giant sealed envelope without tearing it and walking out of jail cells that were said to be escape-proof.

6. Clearly, Houdini did not want anyone to know his secrets.

8. Houdini's tremendous control over almost every muscle allowed him to contort his body into seemingly impossible positions.

10. On his deathbed, Houdini promised his wife that he would try to make contact with her from beyond the grave, but so far, he has never been able to get in touch.

SENTENCE GRAMMAR

EXERCISE 28.1 Identifying subjects and predicates

The subject is set in *italics;* the predicate is set in **boldface.**

2. *It* **was an immense crowd, two thousand at the least and growing every minute.**

4. In a job like that, *you* see the dirty work of Empire at close quarters.

6. *The hangman, a gray-haired convict in the white uniform of the prison,* **was waiting beside his machine.**

8. **Would** *I* **please come and do something about it?**

10. *We* **set out for the gallows.**

EXERCISE 28.2 Identifying verbs and verb phrases

2. Holi <u>is known</u> as the festival of colors, not only because spring <u>brings</u> flowers, but also because Holi celebrations always <u>include</u> brightly colored dyes.

4. During Holi, people <u>toss</u> fistfuls of powdered dyes or dye-filled water balloons at each other and <u>sing</u> traditional Holi songs.

6. Any person who <u>is walking</u> outside during a Holi celebration <u>will</u> soon <u>be wearing</u> colored powders or colored water.

8. Most people <u>wear</u> white clothing for Holi.

10. <u>Doesn't</u> Holi <u>sound</u> like fun?

EXERCISE 28.3 Identifying nouns and articles

Nouns are set in *italics;* articles are set in **boldface.**

2. *Alice; secret*

4. *broccoli; asparagus*

6. *Marlys; reflection;* **the;** *window*

8. *Nightlife; Georgetown;* **the;** *sun*

10. *Journalists; sources;* **a;** *case; security*

EXERCISE 28.4 Identifying pronouns and antecedents

Pronouns are set in *italics;* antecedents are set in **boldface.**

2. **dogs;** *that; their*

4. *they; their;* **volunteers; puppy;** *its*

6. *you;* **puppy;** *its;* **coat;** *that; it*

8. *Some;* **pups;** *these*

10. *you; your*

EXERCISE 28.5 Identifying adjectives and adverbs

Adjectives are set in *italics;* adverbs are set in **boldface.**

2. **agonizingly; slowly; finally**
4. *The;* **somewhat;** *shy;* **reluctantly;** *six; exuberant*
6. *The; youngest; the; a; brilliant*
8. **Never; before;** *one; a; bigger; this*
10. *Imminent; many;* **constantly**

EXERCISE 28.6 Adding adjectives and adverbs

SUGGESTED ANSWERS

2. Surely, most of us enjoy classic movies.
4. A multinational corporation can fire undependable workers.
6. The unpopulated boardwalk crosses the bleak, wintry beach.
8. The mainstream media are determinedly ignoring his candidacy.
10. Which way did you say the hunted pair went yesterday?

EXERCISE 28.7 Identifying prepositions

2. on; into; of
4. to; without
6. In; between; in addition to
8. in; because of; in; of; beyond; of
10. to; from

EXERCISE 28.8 Identifying conjunctions

2. for
4. When
6. Although; and; as though
8. whether . . . or [two parts of a correlative conjunction]; after
10. because

EXERCISE 28.9 Identifying conjunctions and interjections

2. Hey! (interjection); and (COORD)
4. Um (interjection); if (SUBORD)
6. Until (SUBORD)
8. and (COORD); Wow! (interjection)
10. so (COORD)

EXERCISE 28.10 Identifying the parts of speech

2. is selling – verb; cosmetics – noun; attractive – adjective

4. Middle Earth – noun (proper); while – conjunction (subordinating); on – preposition

6. In – preposition; that – pronoun (relative); consistently – adverb; our – pronoun (possessive)

8. also – adverb; safety – noun; that – pronoun (relative)

10. hey – interjection; bought – verb; who – pronoun (relative); the – article (adjective)

EXERCISE 28.11 Identifying subjects

Complete subjects are set in *italics*; simple subjects are set in **boldface.**

2. *Working to "improve" inconvenient or unpoetic facts,* **writers**

4. **writers** *telling a true story*

6. *Today's* **filmmakers**

8. **Shakespeare,** *whose works have recently proved to be a big box-office draw*

10. **Nobody** *in the crowd in a Shakespearean theater*

EXERCISE 28.12 Identifying predicates

Predicates are set in *italics.*

2. *favored* [TV] *capital punishment* [DO]

4. *called* [TV] *capital punishment* [DO] *"cruel and unusual"* [OC] . . . *outlawed* [TV] *it* [DO] *in 1972*

6. *was developed* [IV] *as an alternative to older execution methods such as hanging*

8. *has given* [TV] *more than a hundred prisoners on death row* [IO] *their freedom* [DO]

10. *were* [LV] *the only industrialized nations* [SC] . . . *used* [TV] *the death penalty* [DO]

EXERCISE 28.13 Identifying prepositional phrases

2. in Columbus; like coaching; in New Haven

4. of shoulder; of tread; behind the glittering glasses

Imitations of these sentences will vary.

EXERCISE 28.14   Using prepositional phrases

SUGGESTED ANSWERS

2. Polytetrafluoroethylene (PTFE) is the chemical name for Teflon.

4. The substance allows food to cook in a pan without sticking.

6. Early nonstick cookware coating tended to peel off the surface of the pan at the slightest touch of a metal utensil.

8. The primer holds the PTFE coat in place with a physical bond, not a chemical one.

10. As an adjective, the word *Teflon* describes a person who seems to get out of sticky situations easily.

EXERCISE 28.15   Identifying verbal phrases

2. inf – To check Turing's hypothesis; inf – to determine if any of them can successfully mimic a human conversation

4. part – Programmed for artificial intelligence; inf – to imitate humans in Internet chat rooms

6. gerund, subject – Teaching a machine artificial intelligence

8. gerund, subject – Receiving a $2000 consolation prize

10. gerund – being a computer

EXERCISE 28.16   Identifying prepositional, verbal, absolute, and appositive phrases

2. verbal – outlined against the sky; prep – against the sky; verbal – to move

4. absolute – her fingers clutching the fence; verbal – clutching the fence

6. verbal – Floating on my back; prep – on my back

8. app – the leader of the group; prep – of the group; verbal – to relinquish any authority

10. verbal – Shocked into silence; prep – into silence; verbal – fixed on the odd creature; prep – on the odd creature

EXERCISE 28.17   Adding prepositional, verbal, absolute, and appositive phrases

SUGGESTED ANSWERS

2. Teresa looked at her mother, her eyes searching for the familiar face that now seemed so old.

4. Having thoughtlessly locked ourselves out while the bathtub filled with water, we were uncertain what to do.

6. Gazing out the window, he wondered about the disappearance of the buffalo nickel, replaced by a smaller, less interesting five-cent coin.

8. Unopened, the letter lay on the desk in its gleaming white envelope looking very inviting.

10. Ten hours of sleep, almost twice her usual amount, exhausted her, leaving her head almost too heavy to lift from the pillow.

EXERCISE 28.18 Using verbal, absolute, and appositive phrases to combine sentences

SUGGESTED ANSWERS

2. To lift her spirits, she bought a new camera.

4. David Klein, an actor and comedian, performed a monologue.

6. Concentrating intensely on his experiments, he blocks out the rest of the world.

8. The bird, a gray macaw, allows no one but Julie to come near it.

10. Their banners carried aloft, the protesters headed down the street.

EXERCISE 28.19 Identifying dependent clauses

Dependent clauses are set in *italics*.

2. *when spring arrives in the South;* sub conj–when

4. *Although the Appalachian mountain range has relatively low peaks;* sub conj–Although

6. *Because the Appalachian Trail lies mainly in wilderness;* sub conj–Because

8. *that have become accustomed to humans;* rel pron–that

10. *how to react to an aggressive bear to minimize the danger;* rel pron–how

EXERCISE 28.20 Adding dependent clauses

SUGGESTED ANSWERS

2. Everyone in a family that spends the day in separate places may have high expectations for time together.

4. Whining, which all children do from time to time, is difficult to listen to and easy to stop with a new toy or an extra video viewing.

6. Misbehaving children who expect to get their own way wear out their welcome quickly.

8. Parents who want to set a good example must learn to stick to their own rules.

10. Even if children protest against discipline, which everyone resists from time to time, they want to know how to behave.

EXERCISE 28.21   Distinguishing between phrases and clauses

Dependent clauses are set in *italics*; phrases are set in **boldface**.

2. **as beyond recall, beyond recall** – prep phrases

4. **of encountering a Perelman piece** – prep phrase; **encountering a Perelman piece** – verbal phrase; **in a magazine** – prep phrase

6. **at a glance** – prep phrase; *that Professor Strunk omitted needless words*

8. *When I start a book; what my characters are going to do;* **to do** – verbal; **for their eccentric behavior** – prep phrase

10. *When I wrote "Death of a Pig";* **of a Pig** – prep phrase; **of what actually happened** – prep phrase; **on my place** – prep phrase; **to my pig** – prep phrase; *who died;* **to me** – prep phrase; *who tended him;* **in his last hours** – prep phrase

Imitation sentences will vary.

EXERCISE 28.22   Classifying sentences grammatically and functionally

2. complex, declarative

4. compound-complex, declarative

6. complex, declarative

8. compound, declarative

10. simple, exclamatory

EXERCISE 29.1   Using irregular verb forms

2. was; said; was

4. broke; lay

6. met; fell

8. kept; was

10. grown; spread

EXERCISE 29.2 Editing verb forms

2. freezed—froze

4. ate—eaten

6. Correct

8. knowed—known

10. Correct

EXERCISE 29.3 Distinguishing between *lie* and *lay, sit* and *set, rise* and *raise*

2. raise

4. rose

6. set

8. rose

10. lies

EXERCISE 29.4 Deciding on verb tenses

2. invited

4. was

6. interrogated; died

8. showed / had shown

10. began; became

EXERCISE 29.5 Sequencing tenses

2. Until I *started* knitting again last month, I *had forgotten* how.

4. After Darius said that he wanted to postpone college, I *tried* to talk him out of it.

6. They *had hoped* to plant their garden by now.

8. When he *was* twenty-one, he *wanted* to *become* a millionaire by the age of thirty.

10. *Having cut off* all contact with family, he *did* not *know* whom to ask for help.

EXERCISE 29.6   Converting the voice of a sentence

Answers may vary slightly.

2.   The storm *uprooted* huge pine trees.
4.   Jerry *ate* the last doughnut in the box just a few minutes ago.
6.   For months, the mother kangaroo *protects, feeds,* and *teaches* its baby how to survive.
8.   The first snow of winter *covered* the lawns and rooftops.
10.   Suddenly, the roof over our heads *was being pounded on* by rainfall.

EXERCISE 29.7   Using subjunctive mood

2.   Correct
4.   would have heard—had heard
6.   knows—know
8.   should not take—not take
10.   was—were

EXERCISE 30.1   Selecting verbs that agree with their subjects

2.   are
4.   include
6.   offer
8.   looks
10.   does

EXERCISE 30.2   Making subjects and verbs agree

2.   are—is
4.   use—uses
6.   sets—set
8.   Correct
10.   allows—allow
12.   Correct
14.   belongs—belong

EXERCISE 31.1 Using adjectives and adverbs appropriately

2. defiant—defiantly; modifies *crosses*
4. sadly—sad; modifies *you*
6. relievedly—relieved; modifies *you*
8. oddly—odd; modifies *"words"*
10. Lucky—Luckily; modifies *available*

EXERCISE 31.2 Using comparative and superlative modifiers appropriately

SUGGESTED ANSWERS

2. to live longer—to live longer than men
4. the largest—the larger
6. the famousest—the most famous
8. unpleasantest—most unpleasant
10. the most unique—a unique

EXERCISE 32.1 Revising sentences with misplaced modifiers

SUGGESTED ANSWERS

2. Singing with verve, the tenor captivated the entire audience.
4. The city spent approximately twelve million dollars on the new stadium.
6. On the day in question, the patient was not able to breathe normally.
8. The clothes that I was giving away were full of holes.
10. A wailing baby with a soggy diaper was quickly kissed by the candidate.

EXERCISE 32.2 Revising squinting modifiers, disruptive modifiers, and split infinitives

SUGGESTED ANSWERS

2. He vividly remembered enjoying the sound of Mrs. McIntosh's singing.
4. The mayor promised that after her reelection she would not raise taxes.

   After her reelection, the mayor promised that she would not raise taxes.
6. The collector who originally owned the painting planned to leave it to a museum.

The collector who owned the painting planned originally to leave it to a museum.

8. Doctors can now restore limbs that have been partially severed to functioning condition.

   Doctors can now restore limbs that have been severed to a partially functioning condition.

10. The speaker said he would answer questions when he finished.

    When he finished, the speaker said he would answer questions.

12. After a long summer under the blazing sun, the compost smelled pretty bad when I turned it.

14. After a long day at work and an evening class, Stella did not want to argue about who was going to do the dishes.

    Stella did not want to argue about who was going to do the dishes after a long day at work and an evening class.

EXERCISE 32.3 Revising dangling modifiers

SUGGESTED ANSWERS

2. When interviewing grieving relatives, reporters show no consideration for their privacy.

4. Chosen for their looks, newscasters often have weak journalistic credentials.

6. Assuming that viewers care about no one except Americans, editorial boards for network news shows reject many international stories.

8. Horrified by stories of bloodshed, most viewers don't recognize the low probability of becoming the victim of crime or terrorism.

10. Not covering less sensational but more common dangers such as reckless driving and diabetes, news broadcasts do not tell viewers what is really likely to hurt them.

12. Reporting on a national story, journalists may focus on speculation about causes instead of on what actually happened.

14. Whether political discussions are on talk radio or on political talk shows on television, distortions and bias are the norm.

EXERCISE 33.1 Using subjective case pronouns

2. they
4. they
6. they
8. We
10. she

EXERCISE 33.2 Using objective case pronouns

2. Correct
4. When we asked, the seller promised <u>us</u> that the software would work on a Macintosh computer.
6. Max told Jackson and him that the cabin was available to <u>them</u>.
8. Correct
10. We need two volunteers: <u>you</u> and Tom.

EXERCISE 33.3 Using possessive case pronouns

2. mine
4. Her
6. their
8. her
10. yours

EXERCISE 33.4 Using *who, whoever, whom,* or *whomever*

2. Whomever
4. whoever
6. Whom
8. whom
10. whoever

EXERCISE 33.5 Using pronouns in compound structures, appositives, elliptical clauses; choosing between *we* and *us* before a noun

2.	he	10.	he
4.	he	12.	us
6.	her	14.	I
8.	them		

EXERCISE 33.6 Maintaining pronoun-antecedent agreement

SUGGESTED ANSWERS

2. A child-free person may feel that people with children see his or her time as less valuable than their own.

4. Child-free employees may feel that they have to subsidize family medical plans at work for people who have children.

6. However, a community has to consider the welfare of its children because caring for and educating children eventually benefits everyone.

8. Almost no one would be able to afford to have children if parents were expected to pay for educating and training their offspring entirely without help.

10. As writer Barbara Kingsolver once pointed out, even people without children will probably need the services of a doctor or a mechanic in their old age.

EXERCISE 33.7 Clarifying pronoun reference

SUGGESTED ANSWERS

2. Not long after the company set up the subsidiary, the subsidiary went bankrupt.

    Not long after the company set up the subsidiary, the company went bankrupt.

4. When Deyon was reunited with his father, the boy wept.

    When Deyon was reunited with his father, his father wept.

6. The weather forecast said to expect snow in the overnight hours.

8. Lear divides his kingdom between the two older daughters, Goneril and Regan, whose extravagant professions of love are more flattering than the simple affection of the youngest daughter, Cordelia. The consequences of this error in judgment soon become apparent, as the older daughters prove neither grateful nor kind to him.

10. The visit to the pyramids was canceled because of the recent terrorist attacks on tourists there, so Kay, who had waited years to see the monuments, was disappointed.

EXERCISE 34.1 Revising comma splices and fused sentences

Only one suggested answer is given for each numbered item.

2. The group Human Rights Watch filed a report on Mauritania, a nation in northwest Africa.

4. Members of Mauritania's ruling group are called the Beydanes, an Arab Berber tribe also known as the White Moors.

6. In modern-day Mauritania, many of the Haratin are still slaves; they serve the Beydanes.

8. Mauritania outlawed slavery in 1981, but little has been done to enforce the law.

10. Physical force is not usually used to enslave the Haratin. Rather, they are held by the force of conditioning.

12. By some estimates 300,000 former slaves, who are psychologically and economically dependent, still serve their old masters.

14. In addition, there may be as many as 90,000 Haratin still enslaved; some Beydanes have refused to free their slaves unless the government pays compensation.

16. Of course, slavery must have existed in Mauritania, or there would have been no compelling reason to make a decree to abolish it in 1981.

18. Both the slaveholding Beydanes and the enslaved Haratin are made up largely of Muslims, so some people in Mauritania see resistance to slavery in their country as anti-Muslim.

20. Islamic authorities in Mauritania have agreed that all Muslims are equal; therefore, one Muslim must not enslave another.

EXERCISE 35.1 Eliminating sentence fragments

SUGGESTED ANSWERS

2. Her father pulled strings to get her the job. Later he regretted his actions.

4. I must have looked ridiculous trying to carry a portfolio, art box, illustration boards, and drawing pads.

6. Connie picked up the cat and started playing with it. It scratched her neck with its sharp little claws.

8. The region has dry, sandy soil, blown into strange formations by the ever-present wind.

10. Many older Americans want nothing more than to feel useful.

LANGUAGE/GLOSSARY OF USAGE

EXERCISE 37.1 Identifying stereotypes

2. *how few hours:* Overlooks all the other work academics do in addition to classroom teaching: grading, conferencing, committee work, research.

4. *everyone in France hates Americans:* Overlooks the fact that like people everywhere, people in France are individuals with widely varying points of view about Americans (and every other topic).

6. *Dropouts:* Assumes anyone who didn't finish high school chose not to finish and is therefore foolish, unmotivated, lazy, or (perhaps) a criminal.

8. *ambulance chasers:* Assumes that lawyers are frivolous and out to earn large fees in order to benefit from the pain of others.

EXERCISE 37.3   Rewriting to eliminate offensive references

SUGGESTED ANSWERS

2. All of the children in the kindergarten class will ask someone at home to help make cookies for the bake sale.

4. Acting as a spokesperson, Cynthia McDowell vowed that all elementary schoolteachers in the district would take their turns on the picket line until the school board agreed to resume negotiations.

6. Violinist Josh Mickle, last night's featured soloist, brought the crowd to its feet. (Or accept any version that omits mention of age and religion—both irrelevant here.)

8. Despite the plane's mechanical problems, the crew members were able to calm the passengers and land safely.

10. Attorney Margaret Samuelson won her sixteenth case in a row last week.

EXERCISE 39.1   Using formal register

SUGGESTED ANSWERS

2. The young dancers stamped their feet so that their anklets jingled, and the audience watched them approvingly.

4. We decided not to buy a bigger car that got terrible gas mileage and instead to keep our old Honda.

6. After she had raced to the post office at ten minutes to five, she realized that she had completely forgotten the fact that it was a federal holiday.

8. Moby Dick's enormous size was matched only by Ahab's obsessive desire to destroy him.

10. The class misbehaved so dreadfully in their regular teacher's absence that the substitute lost his temper.

EXERCISE 39.2   Determining levels of language

SUGGESTED ANSWERS

2. formal; *audience:* a prospective employer you want to impress

4. formal; *audience:* an informed audience whom you hope to convince

EXERCISE 39.3   Checking for correct denotation

2. apex; Correct word: nadir [or "low point"]

4. effected; Correct word: affected

6. Correct

8. delusion; Correct word: illusion

10. <u>Retrofitting</u>; Correct word: Reintroducing

EXERCISE 39.4   Revising sentences to change connotations

2. waltz away/little people who keep the company running/peanuts

    Rewrite: CEOs are highly compensated with salary, stock options, and pension funds while employees get comparatively little.

4. Tree-huggers/ranted

    Rewrite: Environmentalists protested the Explorer's gas mileage outside the Ford dealership.

6. Naive/stumble/blithely yank

    Rewrite: Often voters not familiar with using a voting machine will simply pull the handle without making informed choices.

8. mob/yelling/jabbing

    Rewrite: A large group of chanting, sign-waving protesters appeared.

EXERCISE 39.5   Considering connotation

SUGGESTED ANSWERS

2. *girl:* young lady, miss

4. *abide:* tolerate; *turns:* changes; *vital:* alive; *hold still:* contain their energy

EXERCISE 39.6   Using specific and concrete words

SUGGESTED ANSWERS

2. He has stained and crooked teeth, small eyes, and a few stray hairs that he considers a mustache on his upper lip, but he tells wonderful stories and has an enormous store of knowledge ranging from anthropology to political progressivism.

4. The Smollings' children rarely get invited to other peoples' homes because they squabble constantly, demand endless adult attention, break dishes, and jump on furniture.

6. Robert had a fever of 103 degrees and a rasping cough, so he stayed home from the holiday party at his office.

8. The feast at Mom's on Sunday was delicious as usual: roast chicken, garlic and sage stuffing, sweet garden peas, gallons of gravy, and half a fresh-baked apple pie each.

10. Few places in the United States display the wild climatic variations of central Texas: at one moment, the sky may be clear blue and the air balmy; at another, a racing flash flood may drown the landscape and threaten lives.

EXERCISE 39.7 Thinking about similes and metaphors

SUGGESTED ANSWERS

2. *great mounds of marshmallow fluff* (metaphor): clarifies the white and fluffy appearance of the clouds

4. *as if someone had punched him in the stomach* (simile): compares an emotion with a physical feeling

6. *like a magnolia corsage* (simile): makes vivid and concrete Mom Willie's heritage and suggests how positively she values it—and how proudly she "displays" it

8. *deep and soft like water moving in a cavern* (simile): compares the sound of her voice to water in a cavern, helping the reader to imagine the sound

10. *lounging* (metaphor): compares the horse in pasture to people relaxing; *cuddling up* (metaphor): emphasizes the pleasure the writer has reading mysteries; *top priority* (metaphor): reading as an activity of official importance

EXERCISE 40.1 Recognizing correct spellings

2. sense
4. apparently; harass
6. which; accepted
8. especially
10. know; profit

EXERCISE 40.4 Spelling plurals

2. phenomena
4. media
6. crutches
8. stepchildren
10. babies
12. sergeants-at-arms

EXERCISE 41.1 Selecting the appropriate word

2. disinterested
4. allude
6. reason
8. raises
10. quotation
12. flaunted
14. outside
16. principals
18. than
20. every day

EXERCISE 41.2   Editing inappropiate words

2. Correct

4. Johanna *hung* the sheets on the line because the fresh air made them smell good, but the neighbors complained.

6. The supervisor and the trainee speak to each other *every day*.

8. Correct

10. A small *percentage* of the graduates weren't qualified for the entry-level positions.

12. Swiss cheese is *different from* Jarlsberg.

14. Correct

16. She *immigrated* to New York in the 1920s.

18. My visiting relatives made *themselves* look like tourists by wearing white sneakers and by staring at all of the tall buildings.

20. *It's hoped* that it won't rain during the company outing.

   OR

   We hope that it won't rain during the company outing.

PUNCTUATION/MECHANICS

EXERCISE 42.1   Using a comma to set off introductory elements

2. In the past,

4. Of course,

6. Someday,

8. Naturally,

10. Unable to judge whether smells are delectable or nauseating,

EXERCISE 42.2   Using a comma in compound sentences

SUGGESTED ANSWERS

2. Over two decades ago, fertility treatments were a little-explored field, *so* the first "test-tube baby" astonished the world.

4. A scientist combines an egg cell and a sperm cell, *and* an embryo forms when the egg cell begins to divide.

6. The procedure requires scientific intervention, *yet* the parents of a "test-tube baby" have a child that is biologically theirs.

8. In vitro fertilization has helped many people have children, *but* it is expensive.

10. The first "test-tube baby," who was born in England, was a celebrity, *but* today, children whose parents used in vitro fertilization are quite common.

EXERCISE 42.3   Recognizing restrictive and nonrestrictive elements

2. The clause *that preserves a cadaver* is essential for the sentence to have any meaning at all. Therefore, it should not take commas.

4. Do not set off the phrase *standing in the hall outside the classroom,* or readers will not know which girl is meant.

6. The appositive phrase *reading Web logs* is not needed to make the meaning of the sentence clear. It should be set off with commas.

8. The appositive that describes Karl Marx is providing additional but not essential information. Therefore, *an important nineteenth-century political philosopher* should be set off from the rest of the sentence.

10. The phrase *an ancient tribe* provides additional information and should be set off from the rest of the sentence with commas.

12. The participial phrase *made of wood* is restrictive because the meaning of the sentence is not complete without it. That the houses are made of wood is what often allows them to survive earthquakes. Therefore, the phrase should not take commas.

14. The clause *who rescued her puppy* is restrictive because only the man who rescued the puppy won the gratitude. The winning of eternal gratitude is restricted to the man who rescued the puppy. Therefore, the clause should not take commas.

EXERCISE 42.4   Using commas to set off items in a series

2. I am looking forward to turning eighteen, being able to vote, and perhaps serving in the military.

4. The moon circles the earth, the earth revolves around the sun, and the sun is just one star among many in the Milky Way galaxy.

6. Correct

8. The firm's quiet, pleasant, excessively polite public relations executives made everyone a little nervous.

10. Superficial observation does not provide accurate insight into people's lives—how they feel, what they believe in, how they respond to others.

EXERCISE 42.5   Using commas to set off parenthetical and transitional expressions, contrasting elements, interjections, direct address, and tag questions

2. Madame President, I move to adjourn the meeting.

4. The West, in fact, has become solidly Republican in presidential elections.

6. Captain Kirk, I'm a doctor, not a madman.

8. One must consider the society as a whole, not just its parts.

10. Mary announced, "Kids, I want you to clean your rooms, not make a bigger mess."

EXERCISE 42.6 Using commas with dates, addresses, titles, numbers, and quotations

2. Correct

4. "Who can match the desperate humorlessness of the adolescent who thinks he is the first to discover seriousness?" asks P. J. Kavanaugh.

6. The ship was hit by two torpedoes on May 7, 1915, and sank in minutes.

8. "Neat people are lazier and meaner than sloppy people," according to Suzanne Britt.

10. Correct

EXERCISE 42.7 Eliminating unnecessary and inappropriate commas

2. Insomniacs do indeed wake up at night, but studies have demonstrated that they also have trouble napping during the day.

4. In many cases, insomniacs suffer from anxiety.

6. Correct

8. Sleep therapists recommend going to bed at the same time every night, not watching television in bed, and not reading in bed.

10. While tired people are more dangerous drivers and less productive workers, no one knows for certain if insomnia can actually make them sick.

EXERCISE 43.1 Using semicolons to link clauses

2. Teenagers today don't spend all their time on the telephone; instead, they go online and send each other instant messages.

4. The unwanted package arrived C.O.D.; I politely refused to pay the charges.

6. Pittsburgh was once notorious for its smoke and grime; today, its skies and streets are cleaner than those of many other American cities.

8. Establishing your position in an office is an important task; your profile will mold your relationships with other staff members.

10. Florida's mild winter climate is ideal for bicycling; in addition, the terrain is very flat.

EXERCISE 43.2 Eliminating misused semicolons

2. Verbal scores have decreased by more than fifty-four points, while math scores have decreased by more than thirty-six.

4. Finally, I found her at the Humane Society: a beautiful shepherd-collie mix who likes children and plays well with cats.

6. He left a large estate, which was used to endow a scholarship fund.

8. You can't take your ball and go home just because you think you'll lose the game.

10. The speech made sense to some observers, but not to me.

EXERCISE 44.1 Using periods appropriately

2. She has raised disturbing questions about why parents sometimes kill their offspring.

4. Human parents, even in recent centuries, may actively or passively have limited their children's chances to grow up.

6. The term "parent-offspring conflict" was coined by Robert Trivers, PhD.

8. Many mothers are indeed willing to put up with a great deal from their children, from 2:00 a.m. feedings through requests for college tuition.

10. Describing a mother's crime against her child as "inhuman" is neither accurate nor helpful in preventing future tragedies.

EXERCISE 44.2 Using question marks appropriately

2. "Can I play this?" asked Manuel.

4. "How long are we supposed to wait for Sara?" wondered Erin.

6. Correct

8. Correct

10. The judge asked, "What is your verdict?"

EXERCISE 44.3 Using exclamation points appropriately

SUGGESTED ANSWERS

2. Oh no! We've lost the house!

4. "Go! Go! Go!" roared the crowd as the quarterback sped toward the end zone.

6. It was an ordinary school day, so the child once again came home to an empty house.

8. She exclaimed, "It's too hot!"

10. "This is ridiculous!" sputtered the diner as the waiter brought the wrong order again.

EXERCISE 45.1 Using apostrophes to signal possession

2. Recipients who pass on messages want everyone to hear about a *child's* inspiring fight against cancer or about some dangerous drug, product, or disease.

4. A *hoax's* creators count on *recipients'* kind hearts and concern for the well-being of their families and friends.

6. Have you heard the one about how *deodorants'* ingredients supposedly clog your pores and cause cancer?

8. Some of these scares are probably intended to damage certain *corporations'* reputations by spreading rumors about products.

10. The *Internet's* speed has made such anonymous rumors spread more rapidly than anyone would have thought possible twenty years ago.

EXERCISE 45.2 Using apostrophes to create contractions

2. I can't believe you haven't started the paper yet; it's due tomorrow morning.

4. That guy who's been giving you a ride after work called at about nine o'clock.

6. The clothes that I'm washing now didn't really get too dirty.

8. The distributor says that your order hasn't received its approval from the business office.

10. Isn't that the new jazz club that's open on weekends?

EXERCISE 46.1 Using quotation marks to signal direct quotations

2. Correct

4. To repeat their words, "The worst is behind us."

6. Correct

8. "I could not believe the condition of my hometown," he wrote.

10. "Is the computer plugged in?" the technical support operator asked, prompting Harry to snarl, "Yes, I'm not a complete idiot."

EXERCISE 46.2 Using quotation marks for definitions and titles

2. My dictionary defines *isolation* as "the quality or state of being alone."

4. Kowinski uses the term *mallaise* to mean "physical and psychological disturbances caused by mall contact."

6. "The little that is known about gorillas certainly makes you want to know more," writes Alan Moorehead in his essay "A Most Forgiving Ape."

8. If you had ever had "Stairway to Heaven" running through your head for four days straight, you would not like Led Zeppelin either.

10. Amy Lowell challenges social conformity in her poem "Patterns."

EXERCISE 46.3 Using quotation marks appropriately

SUGGESTED ANSWERS

2. Television commercials have frequently used popular songs as an effective way to connect their product with good feelings in consumers' minds.

4. The strategy of using hit songs in commercials can backfire when the listeners don't like the song or like it too much to think of it as an advertising jingle.

6. The rights to many Beatles songs, such as "Revolution," are no longer controlled by the Beatles.

8. Many Iggy Pop fans wonder what on earth his song "Lust for Life" has to do with taking an expensive ocean cruise.

10. Do consumers love the songs of their youth so much that merely hearing a song in an ad will make them buy that car?

EXERCISE 47.1 Using parentheses and brackets

2. Are the media really elite, and are they really liberal, as talk-show regulars (Ann Coulter, for example) argue?

4. An article in the *Journal of Communication* discussing the outcome of recent U.S. elections explained that "claiming the media are liberally biased perhaps has become a core rhetorical strategy" used by conservatives (qtd. in Alterman 14).

6. However, liberals are not the only media watchdogs: right-wing organizations, including Accuracy in Media (AIM), also closely examine the way political stories are reported.

8. According to the site's home page, the purpose of Campaign Desk was "to straighten and deepen campaign coverage" as a resource for voters (most of whom rely on media coverage to make decisions about the candidates).

10. And can we forget that as media consumers, we have an obligation to be an informed electorate (even though it's easy to pay attention only to the news that reinforces our own beliefs)?

EXERCISE 47.2 Using dashes

2. Nevertheless, extra charges seem to be added to more and more services all the time.

4. The hidden costs of service fees are irritating—people feel that their bank accounts are being nibbled to death.

6. The "convenience charges" that people have to pay when buying show tickets by telephone are often a substantial percentage of the cost of the ticket.

8. Correct

10. Correct

EXERCISE 47.3 Using colons

2. Correct

4. The sonnet's structure is effective in revealing the speaker's message: love has changed his life and ended his depression.

6. Even more important was what money represented: success, prestige, and power.

8. Correct

10. Reviewers agree that Lisa's book possesses these traits: readability, intelligence, and usefulness.

EXERCISE 47.5 Reviewing punctuation marks

SUGGESTED ANSWERS

2. Some parental efforts do help children; for instance, children whose parents read to them are more likely to enjoy books.

4. A new idea that is popular with many parents of young children is sign language.

6. By sixteen to eighteen months, most children are able to speak simple words and make themselves understood.

8. Garcia showed that parents could easily teach their children signs for words like *please, more, sleepy,* and *hungry.*

10. Not surprisingly, parents bought the book (and then the video), and now sign-language classes for small children are easy to find.

12. Correct

14. The researchers who developed the study said that the best reason for parents to sign with their children was to allow the children "to communicate what they need and see."

16. Others contend that the children's hand movements stand for concepts, so the movements are sign language.

18. In fact, children who can use sign language are often especially eager to learn how to speak.

20. Any activity that gets parents to spend more time communicating with their children probably has its benefits.

EXERCISE 48.1 Capitalizing

2. The Battle of Lexington and Concord was fought in April 1775.

4. Accepting an award for his score for the film *The High and the Mighty*, Dmitri Tiomkin thanked Beethoven, Brahms, Wagner, and Strauss.

6. We drove east over the Hudson River on the Tappan Zee Bridge.

8. "Bloody Sunday" was a massacre of Catholic protesters in Derry, Northern Ireland, on January 30, 1972.

10. The town in the American South where I was raised had a statue of a Civil War soldier in the center of Main Street.

EXERCISE 49.1 Using abbreviations

2. The power tools, ordinarily used for sanding wood, are placed on a thirty-foot track and plugged in; the sander to reach the end first wins.

4. There are three divisions of belt sander races: the stock division, which races sanders right out of the box; the modified division, which allows any motor the owner wants to add; and the decorative division, which provides a creative outlet for sander owners.

6. The fastest sanders run on very coarse sandpaper—a number sixteen grit is an excellent choice if it's available.

8. The S-B Power Tool Co. in Chicago, maker of Bosch sanders, allows participants to race its tools, but the company does not underwrite races.

10. No one knows what percentage of the nation's power tools have been used for this kind of entertainment.

EXERCISE 49.2 Spelling out numbers and using figures

SUGGESTED ANSWERS

2. You could travel around the city for only sixty-five cents. (*Or* Correct)

4. Correct

6. Correct (*Or* 25 cents)

8. Three hundred seven miles long and eighty-two miles wide, the island offered little of interest.

10. The department received 1,633 calls and 43 letters.

EXERCISE 50.1   Using italics

2. Regional writers produced some American classics, such as Mark Twain's *Huckleberry Finn* and James Fenimore Cooper's *Last of the Mohicans*.

4. Some of the most prolific regional writers were women like Kate Chopin, who wrote her first collection of short stories, *Bayou Folk*, to help support her family.

6. Chopin also departed from regional works to explore women's experiences of marriage, as in her short piece, "The Story of an Hour."

8. She later turned these into a novel, *Deephaven*, which she hoped would "teach the world that country people were not . . . ignorant."

10. Many regional stories—Stephen Crane's "The Bride Comes to Yellow Sky" is a prime example—show the writer's concern that an isolated culture is in danger of disappearing.

EXERCISE 51.1   Using hyphens in compounds and with prefixes

2. thirty-three

4. a politician who is fast-talking (*Fast-talk* is commonly found in dictionaries; thus hyphenation is correct even though the compound adjective comes after the noun.)

6. a what-me-worry look

8. self-guided

10. Correct

EXERCISE 51.2   Using hyphens appropriately

2. The name of the president-elect had been announced an hour before the polls closed.

4. Correct

6. In Bizet's *Carmen*, the ill-fated Carmen is betrayed by her fickleness.

8. The badly wrapped sandwich oozed mustard and bits of soggy lettuce.

10. One of Baryshnikov's favorite dancers was none other than Fred Astaire.

FOR MULTILINGUAL WRITERS

EXERCISE 64.2 Using appropriate determiners; stating plural forms explicitly

2. Dangerous germs such as salmonella are commonly found in some foods.

4. Many people regularly clean their kitchen counters and cutting boards to remove bacteria.

6. Every time someone wipes a counter with a dirty sponge, more germs are spread around the kitchen.

8. According to research studies, young single men's kitchens tend to have fewer germs than other kitchens.

10. To eliminate many dangerous bacteria from the kitchen, cooks should wash their hands frequently.

EXERCISE 64.4 Positioning modifiers

2. large deserted amusement park

4. valuable multivolume encyclopedia

6. coed volleyball team

8. worthwhile educational program

10. X-rated movie rental

EXERCISE 65.2 Using specified forms of verbs

SUGGESTED ANSWERS

2. Someone followed the instructions too literally.
   Someone was following us as we drove to the beach.

4. The geese migrated to avoid a harsh winter.
   The geese are migrating late this year.

6. Those teenagers consumed three dozen hamburgers and two cases of pop.
   When I left the picnic, the teenagers were consuming the last of the carrot cake.

8. The pasta steamed in the buffet tray.
   The pasta is steaming up the kitchen.

10. This hamburger tastes good.
    The hamburger had tasted fine until I noticed the fly on the bun.

EXERCISE 65.3   Identifying tenses and forms of verbs

2. were talking: past progressive
4. were arriving: past progressive; was getting: past progressive
6. have attempted: present perfect
8. has driven: present perfect
10. had forgotten: past perfect

EXERCISE 65.4   Using verbs appropriately

2. The Rosetta Stone is *covered* with inscriptions in three ancient languages.
4. At that time, scholars *had been* puzzled by hieroglyphics for centuries.
6. A scholar named Jean François Champollion could *understand* both ancient Greek and modern Egyptian, known as Coptic.
8. From the Coptic inscription, he *learned* to read the hieroglyphics.
10. The hieroglyphics, Demotic, and Greek texts all *contain* a decree from an ancient king.

EXERCISE 66.1   Using prepositions idiomatically

2. in/during
4. in
6. on
8. with
10. to

EXERCISE 66.2   Recognizing and using two-word verbs

2. two-word verb
4. two-word verb
6. verb + preposition
8. two-word verb
10. two-word verb

EXERCISE 67.1   Expressing subjects and objects explicitly

SUGGESTED ANSWERS

2. Correct

4. There are problems with doing everything online, of course.

6. There are small-time thieves and juvenile pranksters disrupting online services.

8. A hacker can get enormous amounts of online data, even if it is supposed to be secure.

10. Internet users must use caution and common sense online, but it is also essential for online information to be safeguarded by security experts.

EXERCISE 67.2   Editing for English word order

SUGGESTED ANSWERS

2. He displays a flag proudly in the window.

   OR

   He proudly displays a flag in the window.

4. She should not go into the woods alone.

6. Sandy drove extremely poorly during her first road test.

8. Some restaurant guests would like to begin with desserts.

10. "Speak English fluently," ordered the instructor.

EXERCISE 67.3   Using noun clauses, infinitives, and gerunds appropriately

SUGGESTED ANSWERS

2. We discussed going to a movie, but we could not agree on what to see.

4. Correct

6. Her mother stopped driving on her ninetieth birthday.

8. Correct

10. We appreciated getting the invitation.

EXERCISE 67.4   Using adjective clauses carefully

SUGGESTED ANSWERS

2. Some students who want to practice speaking more asked us all to help prepare a dinner.

4. A reporter attended the dinner and wrote an article in which he praised the chefs.

6. My mother makes many delicious dishes that come from our homeland.

8. We all come from different places, so those of us who were cooking together had to speak English to communicate.

10. Correct

EXERCISE 67.5 Writing conditional sentences

SUGGESTED ANSWERS

2. If the dot-com boom had continued, that prediction might have come true.

4. If any computer job is announced these days, hundreds of qualified people apply for it.

6. If Indian workers required as much money as Americans do to live, U.S. companies would not be as eager to outsource computer work to the other side of the world.

8. Would fewer Americans be unemployed right now if the dot-com boom had never happened?

10. If American students want to prepare for a secure future, they should consider a specialty like nursing, in which jobs are available and the work cannot be sent abroad.